BEYOND MANAGEMENT

Humanizing the Administrative Process

Aldridge
Macy
Walz

Cover by: Carol North   Original illustrations by: Mike Lawler

Library of Congress Cataloging in Publication Data
Aldridge, 1941–
    Beyond Management
    Bibliography: p.
    Includes index.
    1. Social work administration. 2. Social work
administration--United States. I. Macy, 1939–
II. Walz, Thomas, 1933–   III. Title.
HV41.A417   361.3'068   81–19672
ISBN 0-87414-025-0   AACR2

CONTENTS

"In order to produce healthy people, institutions must be
designed specifically to fulfill our basic human needs."

Robert Thomas

Beyond Marriage and

the Nuclear Family

PREFACE

We frail human beings grasp tightly the truths we need and
hold dear the myths that soothe us. None of these myths is more
hallowed to us than the Great American Myth that the individual is
in complete control of his/her own life. Ignoring all the evidence
that constantly taunts us that this myth is not true, each of us
loudly proclaims (without the sarcasm intended by the author) that
"I am the master of my fate; I am the captain of my soul."[1]

Nowhere is there more obvious dissonance between the myth
of individual determination and the reality of restrictions on
our lives than in our functioning in bureaucratic organizations.
When we dream of goals we will reach, when we study to acquire
the skills and knowledge we need to reach the goals, when we work
within organizations to realize these goals--in short, when we
take a rational approach to being "successful" in formal organizations,
we all too often ignore the restrictions placed on us by the nature of
bureaucracy itself. The foreman supervising the construction of a
utility plant makes suggestions that would improve the quality of the
building at the same time that it would decrease costs. He is rewarded
with a curt "That's not your job." A second grade teacher involves
her entire class in the construction of a rocket that will "take
them to the moon." The children grapple with group problem solving,
planning, measurement, cooperation--but the project has to be dropped

when the principal insists, "these competencies are not addressed until fourth grade. Concentrate on the units the School Board has set forth for second graders."

Our reactions to the stifling nature of bureaucratic organization vary, but the authors have found that there are some commonalities. The three of us experienced this reaction with emotions common to culture shock.

For Tom Walz, the sense of a social neurosis began during a period of reverse culture shock.

> In the early 1960's, I lived and worked in the small
> Central American Republic of Honduras as a part of a
> small U.S. contingent of Peace Corps. By mid-1960's
> I had returned to the University of Minnesota to begin
> a career as a social work educator. I can vividly recall
> my first days on the West Bank of the campus where I
> was introduced to the many facets of a multi-university.
> While I had anticipated a modest period of adjustment,
> the culture shock that took place created such tensions
> that it became necessary to order my feelings and
> perceptions. There was something ominous about being
> in an environment which operated on such scale--the
> hundreds of students whose names I would never come to
> know or remember, the faculty colleagues who remained
> little more than a set of distant secondary impressions,
> the morass of rules and regulations which only the well-
> seasoned bureaucrats would come to understand, and even

the buildings which stood out in their austere barrenness
suggesting little personality or character.

Admittedly, the campus had its charm. There were the
small, but meaningful incidents of humanity; the minor
attempts of rebels to push through the standardized
plasticity of the environment. For the most part,
however, the corporate system of multi-university
produced its own life style to which most of its participants
would eventually adapt. The fresh, excited minds and
emotions of newcomers would gradually give way to controlled
attitudes and manipulative behaviors.

Harry Macy's reaction to bureaucratic organization has also been
tempered by bi-cultural experiences:

As an American teacher in Tanzania during the Mid-60's,
I participated in the nationalizing of an H.H. Agakhan
upper primary school. Experiencing the impact of this
type of change increased my awareness of the dynamics
or organizational change--changes in roles, work
relationships, value orientations, staff patterns.
Efforts to blend indigenous religious beliefs and customs
with nationalistic values and newly evolving institutional
structures caused faculty, students, parents and educational
officers alike to undergo adjustments in practically
every facet of their work relationships in an effort
to make the school a viable unit. This was a unique

iii

reorganization experiment designed to retain the local
quality of the education process while at the same time
modifying the education goals of the particular school.
This change occuring in one local school was representative
of a social change design occuring throughout Tanzania
aimed at developing a socialistic society, while retaining
the humanistic qualities of Tribalism. (See Ujamaa by
Julius Neyerere). The outcome of this experiment in social
change is yet undetermined, but the dynamics of organization
change and the effects on people were deeply imbedded in
my mind when I returned to the U.S.

After completing a degree in social work, I obtained
employment in a private family social service agency
located in the inner city of Indianapolis. I experienced
a "turnaround" process of this organization which resulted
in the opening of its doors to serve local neighborhood
families, in addition to the fee-paying middle and upper
income families. As the neighborhood surrounding the
agency changed, low income crisis-oriented families turned
to the agency for an array of social services. These
requests required major reorganizational change at all
levels. As a catalyst for change, I experienced both
the tensions and satisfactions of "opening" the agency
to become a more accessible resource to all families.
Once again, I was reminded of the difficulty of

organizational change, yet remained convinced that change
is possible and improved viability can result.

Lastly, as a faculty member of a university, I have
experienced the usual problems of present day large-scale
educational bureaucracies--communication failures, low
morale, no confidence votes in the administrative offices,
unionization of faculty, ineffective decision-making
process and declining enrollment. As a social work
educator, I am struck with not only the tendency of the
conflictual forces within the organization to overshadow
the apparent strengths and successes, but also the costs
in terms of human suffering to all persons. The seeming
inability of the bureaucracy to "cleanse" itself and
become more open, flexible and accommodating to a diversity
of interests is puzzling. The human costs of the stress
and tensions are tragic.

My interest in the study of organizations centers on
the relationship between the natural organizational
process and the flexible management required to
accommodate diversity within human resources. Are
these unreconcilable differences and are organizations
"naturally" dehumanizing in their basic process? Are
there alternatives?

For Martha Aldridge the experience of culture shock was also precipated by a northward migration to a large midwestern multi-university.

But in my instance, the point of origin was the Gemeinschaft world of the Deep South, where I was accustomed to buying what I needed by writing bank drafts to which I signed my father's name without ever being asked for any proof of my identity (after all, I was born with my identity and everyone I knew, knew me) or proof of approval by him (everyone knew he approved of me). My first confrontation with bureaucratic structure came when I tried to register my car with the University of Wisconsin. Then I learned I did not have a car. My grandmother had given me her Chevrolet--the last major purchase my grandfather had ever made and one which she could not allow to go into the hands of a stranger--but I had no papers to prove that she had given me the car. Four months later when I "officially" owned my car, I was much more sophisticated about the operations of bureaucratic structures, but it has always remained alien to my nature.

For over a decade the three of us, who are now combining our ideas, worked independently, talking with other people in a variety of situations; and we found, as the reader can well imagine, that the frustrations with bureaucratic structures are not limited to those of us who once did not experience such phenomena. In any

classroom, at any party, on any airplane--no matter where--one can
incite lively conversation by bringing up the topic of
"bureaucratic red tape."

We are not sitting down to write about the reaction to bureaucracy
in human service organizations (a reaction we see as neurotic)
and about the American myth of self-determination of the rational
individual to meet his human needs. It is not our purpose to debunk
the myth, but to define the consequences of trying to fulfill human
needs while surviving in bureaucratic organizations. Once the
problem is defined, we set forth a theory of "Humanocracy" and
use this as a framework for action steps by which people can begin
to free bureaucracies to function with human imagination and spirit--
not against it.

Preface Notes

[1]William Ernest Henley, "Invictus."

The first myth of management is that it exists.

Heller's Law

.

CHAPTER I

THE NEUROSIS OF A BUREAUCRATIC SOCIETY

When I try to understand what it is that prevents so many
Americans from being as happy as one might expect, it seems
to me that...one reason is the necessity for subservience
in some large organization. If you are an energetic man with
strong views as to the right way of doing the job with which
you are concerned, you find yourself invariably under the
orders of some big man at the top who is elderly, weary and
cynical. Whenever you have a bright idea, the boss puts a
stopper on it. The more energetic you are and the more vision
you have, the more you will suffer from the impossibility
of doing any of the things that you feel ought to be done.
When you go home and moan to your wife, she tells you that
you are a silly fellow and that if you became the proper sort
of yes-man your income would soon be doubled. If you try
divorce and remarriage it is very unlikely that there will
be any change in this respect. And so you are condemned to
gastric ulcers and premature old age.

Bertrand Russell

Every generation seems to produce its own characteristic neurosis,

and we can boast that we have not failed to color history with

our contribution. We may have emerged from the sexual rigidities

of our Victorian grandparents and the economic anxieties of our

Depression-scarred parents, but we have become a society of people

who spend most of our lives being controlled by organizational

structures that seem to rob us of our humanness. We cling to the

security of rational predictability implicit in bureaucratic organiza-

tions through which we meet needs for food, safety, and status.

The bureaucracies have organized the basic factors of production and distribution of goods in our society to the point that most

Americans have access to dependable resources to meet survival

needs. But the intrinsic controlling nature of bureaucracies compounds

the very insecurities we fight to alleviate.

Much of our society's energy goes into trying to organize

ourselves more efficiently, but as individuals we spend even more

energy trying to beat the system we created ourselves. These rational

bureaucratic structures consistently conflict with our needs to

be human, but we seem unable to break away from our insistence

on maintaining this dissonance. We grimace when another memo comes

across our desk, but we become uneasy when we begin a task without

written approval for spending the necessary money. We acknowledge

verbally that one person can accomplish a task more quickly than

another, but we still will not allow the more efficient worker

to put in less than an eight-hour day. We want our supervisors

to respect our individuality and respond to us as unique human

beings at the same time that we want a contract that guarantees

uniformity in the treatment of all workers who do our job.

Our neurosis is bureau neurosis.

In order to survive in rational but dehumanizing organizations

we have developed a complex psychological adaptation to bureaucracies.

It is from the substance of these reactions that we mold the neurosis

of our generation--a neurosis that we have termed "bureau neurosis."

Bureau neurosis is a complex emotional and behavioral response

of human beings struggling to meet human needs in organizations

that acknowledge the rational components of our personalities.

The totality of the neurosis is made up of six closely interwined reactions:

1. <u>Expectations of Exploitation</u> (the assumption that you will take advantage of me if I don't watch you carefully and keep you from getting the upper hand.)

Whether or not one is actually exploited is irrelevant in our feelings of bureau neurosis. The fact is that everyone involved in the organization acts as if someone will take advantage of them. Would-be rate busters are reticent to perform at full capacity on a day when they feel especially fit and enthusiastic. If they set a precedence of productivity, they might be expected to continue to perform at that level, regardless of variations in their energy level. So, to avoid the risk of being exploited, they work below capacity.

We also insist on rigid adherence to formal job descriptions. Even if there is a rush to prepare a report before a pending deadline, an accountant dares not admit that s/he can type and will not help the typist with the report. The accountant fears being expected to type other documents in the future. Or, if a piece of furniture needs to be moved, we are inclined to wait for a requisition for a maintenance person to wind its way through proper channels rather than move the furniture ourselves. This often repeated cry of "It's not my job!" can be seen as a defense against exploitation.

Nor do we dare become vulnerable to others in the organization. For example, if a company has made a substantial profit and could share it with workers, management may argue against the redistribution on the grounds that workers may come to expect the bonus. Mountains

of restrictions that become part of the tedious "red tape" owe
their existence to our fear of exploitation.

This fear drives us to ally ourselves with others in our category
in the organization and seek the strength of "us" against the power
of "them". Thus we can dichotomize our transactions in organizations
in terms of we/they, workers/management, faculty/administration,
social workers/clients, clerks/customers--we each have our defenses
so that "they" can't exploit "us". If you aren't one of my group,
our relationship is automatically adversarial. The severity of
this feeling of hostility may only be a mild awareness that I must
be alert to the implications of your behavior toward me. Or, there
may be an open hostility that necessitates the addition of mediators
(ombudsmen, union stewards, contract negotiators, etc.) to the
organization..

Even the mildest fear of exploitation contributes to our neurosis
and provides a justification for my exploiting you since you'll
be exploiting me when you have the chance. Such reasoning may
be the explanation for the rise in employee theft, which has been
named as the most critical crime problem facing business. This
expectation of exploitation is certainly the basis for our fear
of dealing with each other openly and honestly. To avoid the slightest
possibility of exploitation, we have developed a host of neurotic
reactions that are a part of bureau neurosis.

2. Not Being (the attempt to be unnoticed by one's superiors
in the organizational structure).

One can certainly argue that it is neurotic for a human being
to attempt to insure "being" by appearing "not to be". The idea
seems strange, yet much of energy in bureaucracies is spent
trying to survive in the system by being invisible. One of the
earliest lessons the novice in the organization learns is that
promotions and other rewards come to those who don't disrupt the
status quo. This includes maintaining a relatively low profile
by following the role prescriptions in all their formalities.
If you can do your job like everyone else who does the same thing,
you increase your chances of not being fired and of being moved
up in the organization through the seniority system. Serving as
a cooperative part of the machinery of the bureaucratic mechanism
is the best insurance for "success" given the reward structure
of the corporate environment. One learns to conform quietly to
the ebb and flow of the organization; for, conformity is rewarded
by promotion. Deviancy, on the other hand, often provides grounds
for dismissal. A scientific analysis of the process of socializing
the individuality out of the individual was provided by Erving
Goffman in Asylums[1]. The process certainly is not restricted only
to such total institutions.

One example of this quiet acceptance and emotional hiding
of self is the tendency to deal with rules by not asking for interpretation. A healthy reaction to a rule to which we cannot
conform may be to question the rationale behind the rule or to
ask for clarification of its meaning. Our neurotic response is
to feign ignorance of the rule or of the boss' interpretation if

we are caught deviating. Such a reaction provides us with the pressure valve needed when we cannot conform, and it allows us to appear ignorant rather than deviant. By appearing not to question the operation of the organization, one has protected the precious facade of not-being.

3. Lack of Trust (the propensity not to trust others until they prove trustworthy).

Most of the energy we expend in bureaucratic organizations is based on our lack of trust of other human beings. We approach situations with the attitude that we must trust our own judgements, but that it is naive to trust others. It seems at times (particularly after a trip to our mail box) that the motto of the bureaucratic organization is "In the memo we trust". We automatically protect ourselves by putting our communications in writing. We would appear foolish and unbusinesslike not to have written documentation of all our actions. If the job doesn't get done, our memos could point out the culprit. When organizations were smaller and people could deal with each other as unique personalities, when a person's reputation as being honest was a matter of pride--then we could relate to each other informally and with less paper. It is not that we moved from the "good old days" of honest people to the new times of people waiting for a chance to cheat or embarrass you. It seems obvious that every era has its crooks and its honest folks. The difference is that now we distrust people until they prove trustworthy. An alternative that was tried before the un-

certainties of the Great Depression was to trust people until they
lost our trust.

4. <u>Lack of Loyalty</u> (consistently placing the needs and wishes of
oneself before the needs of the organization).

Loyalty to the organization has become obsolete. Workers
seek their positions as "a job." Today, managers gain status in
their profession by moving from one company to another. Professors
move from one university to another; workers move to follow the
highest pay and best fringe benefits. The commitment is to one's
self. We only minimally identify with the goals of the organization.
Day after day we spend a substantial amount of time and energy
doing a job to which we have no personal commitment. We move robot-
like through procedures that earn us our checks and our status.
We look with curiousity and some disdain at the "company man."
As one woman said to Studs Terkel, "The only loyal people are the
people who can't get a job elsewhere."[2] Is it any wonder that
our behavior becomes neurotic when we drain most of our human energies
into activities of organizations that have no long-range meanings
for us?

5. <u>Distaste for Work</u> (the separation of self from job and
a dislike of the job because it is our job).

A theme that runs through contemporary literature (both fiction
and non-fiction) is the separation of the persons from the product.
Few of us can take pride in the products of our work. Instead.
work becomes a trial to be endured. We feel interchangeable, not

But the biggest clue seemed to be their expressions.
They were hard to explain. Good-natured, friendly,
easygoing and uninvolved. They were like spectators ...
There was no identification with the job.

       Robert Persig - <u>Zen</u> <u>and</u> <u>the</u> <u>Art</u> <u>of</u>
                          <u>Motorcycle</u> <u>Maintenance</u>

unique. With no commitment to the project, we sense that someone else pays us a flat fee for the services we perform. We do our job; we leave others alone. We feel demeaned, used, owned by the organization. Work is something to escape from, not a challenge to tax our human ingenuity. Those activities that demand so much of our time have become activities that we look on as necessary evils.

6. Denial of Humanness (the attempt to expose our computer-like rationality while hiding our emotions).

The other reactions we see as neurotic seem to form a basis for the existence of another, yet more frightening, neurotic reaction-- the attempt by people in bureaucratic organizations to absent their very spirits from themselves. We relate to others in the organization as role occupants, not as individuals. In fact, we hide our more vulnerable emotional nature lest people get too close. We never share our pain. We make our board presentations with our neatly lined graphs and charts, but with little human passion (except the passion we feign by hours of practice). Bureaucratic organizations become surrealistic with rational, emotionless people moving about, communicating with memos, responding with studied responses. The guts, the daring, the vigor of the human spirit are replaced by the ever-elusive, but ever present goal of controlling oneself and being objective, rational, and sensible. Our world view, as well as our approach to the problems we face in our jobs, becomes closed. There is a "right" answer, and we learn this answer.

Maybe lack of practice, maybe fear of rejection, maybe the whole
rational society itself has made us a generation of people with
the neurotic feeling that being human is not being mature and
responsible.

To summarize, bureau neurosis is the condition that occurs
when individuals learn to survive in the corporate organization,
but only at a heavy cost to their human needs. We are constantly
on the alert not to be taken advantage of, but we do this quietly
and unobstrusively to maintain a low profile. We do our job, careful
not to do anyone else's job, without making waves. Our loyalty
and trust are to ourselves. We don't value other workers as
people, and we don't value our jobs as an expression of ourselves.
We work with others because we need the structure and order that
organization gives us. The organization is only a tool; our jobs
are only what we do to survive. We concentrate on being rational,
efficient, sensible; we shy away from being weak, sad, excited,
loving--from being human.

Survival in the system almost demands this kind of separation
of one's identity and morality from the system. This phenomenon
was described in Working in Welfare: The worker develops hostility
toward bureaucratic personages; "administrators" are not seen as
people; private offices and a personal phone become symbols over
which people are willing to forego friendships. Those who adapt
best are those who learn their lesson best[3]. A frightening part
of our neurosis goes beyond our feeling of being "used" by the

giant machine; we are beginning to seek the security and predictability of the impersonal bureaucratic structure.

This is the neurosis of our time--bureau neurosis. It is neither healthy for the individual nor for society.

Our Society is a Rational Society.

Why do we continue to make choices that create this neurotic behavior? One explanation is that our society values rationality and human integrity almost equally. When we construct our bureaucratic organizations, we emphasize that which reflects rationality; when we work in these organizations, we experience the conflict of rationality over human needs. It is difficult for us to question rational organization for the very reason that it dominates our thinking so consistently. In fact, in American Society, Robin Williams argues that rationality is one of the major values that forms the basis for our decisions[4]. It is a theme that runs through American society, tying cultural elements together and wiping out what had once appeared to be contradictions. When faced with a decision of what action to take on almost any given issue, North Americans are likely to try a choice that "makes sense". This statement is so obvious to us that mention of it seems trite. We are continually being asked to justify our behavior: "Why do you eat candy when you know that it makes you fat, adds blemishes to your face, rots your teeth, and wastes your money?" "Why do you put up with her abuse?" "Why do you lie around in bed when you have so much else to do?" "Why did you spend four years in college if you're only going to go back and work for your father?"

"Why do you study literature when you know it will teach you nothing

that will help you get a better job?" Somehow we expect a rational

answer to each of these questions.

Why do we believe that rational is the natural

way to be? What agents of change have brought us to this point

in social development? Daniel Bell addresses these questions in

The Coming of Post-Industrial Society[5]. He argues that social

change can be understood through the analysis of three "axial

principles" of modern social development. The three principles

(the catalysts for change) are identified as (1) the economizing

principle, (2) the participatory principle, and (3) the self-

actualizing principle. The economizing principle embodies the

concept of rationality. It is essentially an economic principle

which places high value on optimizing production and creating

efficiency and thus stresses goals of maximization, optimization,

standardization, and rationalization.

We embrace this principle because the rationalization of pro-

duction through the use of new machines and organizational technologies

has freed us from arduous labor and speeded up our ability to produce

whatever we are producing at the moment. (Humans are free from

toil, free to contemplate, free to oversee the work and the technology

we have created.) No longer do farmers have to push a heavy plow

behind a sometimes cooperative, sometimes stubborn mule, horse

or ox. Now the farmer rides in an air-conditioned cab of a machine

that can till his land, plant his crops, and harvest his profits.
Today's farmer is a businessman--not a gnarled and weather-beaten
man who looks twice his age.

Women are now free to work in industry, no longer restricted
by the necessity of brute strength or the demands of household
tasks. Machines have freed them to pursue their own identity away
from drudgery.

And technology has brought us health and longevity. We have
drugs that can control our minds, our lives, our hearts, our lungs.
We can even place machines in our hearts and brains that replace
functions which damaged parts of our bodies can no longer perform.
Is it likely that we will abandon the rationality that makes all
this efficient technology available? Of course not. We are constantly
choosing to be rational.

But efficient machines are not enough. Our social institutions
must also be organized efficiently, and the most efficient form
of organization we presently have is bureaucracy. It is considered
as vital as the other basic factors of production, such as a skilled
labor force, raw materials and scientific technology. Consequently,
almost all organizations have adopted this model and religiously
adhere to the bureaucratic form of structure and decision-making.
It is this model of organization that _produces_ in our society.
As Peter Drucker argues:

> A product can only be made if the operations and motions
> of a great many individuals are put together and integrated
> into a pattern. It is this pattern that is actually
> productive, not the individual[6].

This pattern varies according to the character of the individuals ordered by it and according to the goals of the organization, but for the purposes of this book, we are defining bureaucracy in this way:

1. Organizational goals are measured largely, if not exclusively, in terms of the total output (productivity) and the efficiency of that output (cost-effectiveness or profit margin).

2. Organizational objectives are to be operationally specific and quantatively measurable so organizational (and individual) performance evaluations may be objectively conducted.

3. Organizational size is expected to grow to a scale that optimizes the economies of scale.

4. Organizations are expected to be administratively arranged in terms of hierarchy of authority, with clear lines of responsibility and accountability.

5. Authority in organizations is designed as an authority of position (not person) with allegiance and cooperation due to whomever holds the position.

6. The organization is expected to be arranged in terms of specialized functional sub-units, clearly articulated to one another through management control, with specialists assigned to work only within their designated area of specialization.

7. Decision-making and control is expected to be highly centralized with specialists responsible for making data-based, rational decisions.

8. Organizational responsibilities are expected to be specified in terms of clear job descriptions and role prescriptions and to be carried out with total objectivity.

9. All rules, regulations and operations are expected to be standarized, with uniformity of policy and procedure to assure equitable and predictable applications.

10. The organization's physical environment is expected to be designed to optimize efficiency in production and with respect to least cost.

11. Communication within the organization is expected to be written and formal and to follow clearly designated lines of communications.

12. Communication (information) is expected to flow upward in the organization to facilitate top level decision-making; downward communications are to be in the form of directives and prescriptions for further rationalizing bureaucratic behavior.

Such an organizational design is based on and perpetuates the myth that people can be "managed scientifically" as easily as administrators can design organizational charts and write memos. This analysis of man as machine can be traced to Frederick W. Taylor, the "Father of Scientific Management", who gave us, among other

things, a step-by-step breakdown of unloading pig-iron to allow
an analysis of time and technique that would yield that greatest
efficiency and effectiveness. The motivation of the individual
was simply reduced to economic rewards: the worker is very willing
to work for the organization at whatever task and in whatever way
the organization chooses if he can be assured a suitable wage.
Taylor recognized that the worker was not totally as efficient
as a machine. If not consistently overseen by a scientific manager,
he would lapse back into his old, slothful ways.[7]

While it has been over half a century since Taylor began to
publish his work, his assumptions are frighteningly prevalent among
managers in all types of organizations. Granted academics have
turned out volumes of materials of the Hawthorne Study variety
that refute Taylor's simplistic approach to management, but these
studies generally picture contemporary man as more complicated,
but no less mechanical, than Taylor's model.

There has been Douglas McGregor, in whose work the influence
of Maslow can clearly be seen. Man, according to McGregor, will
grow toward self-actualization if given the opportunity.[8] Success
of McGregor's Theory Y approach is documented by Robert Townsend
in Up the Organization.[9] The intensity of Townsend's pleas
and the novelty of his approach is further testimony to the assertion
that ours is still a bureaucratic organized society, at least wishing
to cling to Scientific Management.

This grasping of scientific management as the only alternative
for running organizations is meeting with pressures to change--

pressures brought on by changes in society as a whole. While change
in the post-industrial society has been dominated by what Bell
calls the economizing axial principle, there has been significant,
if less, change in two other principles: the participatory principle
and the principle of self-actualization.[10]

The participatory principle explains change in the political
relations between people in post-industrial society. Basically,
the principle is expressed through various human rights movements
as these efforts move toward a new kind of egalitarianism. Increasingly, people show disdain for hierarchy and privilege. Though
racism, sexism and other forms of discrimination are still widely
practiced, the participatory principle is becoming more important
to us. Many recent developments in human services, namely self-help
movements by consumers and collective bargaining by providers,
owe their impetus to the presence of this principle.

Bell identified the principle of self-actualization as the
prime force in redefining our post-industrial culture. The search
for personal growth and fulfillment (Bell's definition of self-
actualization) has also become an important catalyst behind many
social movements today. While the work world may be characterized
by the economizing principle, our need to be human is defined by
the self-actualizing principle. For this reason (if for no other
reason) we must question whether personal growth and fulfillment
should be sacrificed in the name of either greater production or
greater efficiency.

As Bell points out, and as may be obvious to the reader, these three axial principles are not easily reconciled with each other. Our reactions to scientific management have shown that a strategy of policy decisions based solely on economizing principles creates severe human costs: people who want to help others become "workers" with rigidly defined roles, and human beings who come to us for help become "cases". This transposition has led inevitably to conflict, but the conflict is not between individuals; it is between two mind-sets. The conflict is described by Bell--the inevitable conflict between economizing and self-actualizing. As society has changed, organizations have changed according to Bell's economizing principle. The crisis we experience today is not a crisis precipitated by our inability to manage organizations scientifically; it is a crisis of resisting changes in those very areas in which we are human--areas described by Bell's participatory and self-actualizing principles. It is a crisis because organization has failed to acknowledge that people have a soul, a humaneness. Our art, literature, dance and music have long celebrated this intuitive side of people, but the traditional, rational mind of the scientific manager has tried to ignore it. It is the stuff of literature, the curiosity that drove us to leave this earth for moon and to dream of the time when we can go farther, the will behind Stonehenge and the temples of the Mayans. There is something in people that transcends rationality. We can cry when it doesn't make sense, love when there is not future in it, hate when the hate will destroy us--we can and do behave irrationally, and this intuitive part of our character must be recognized by theories of administration.

No matter how scientifically we study and manage humans, we cannot ignore our human needs. We concur with Drucker's report:

> Every study of workers shows that they consider the social function of the enterprise the most important one. They place the fulfillment of their demands for social status and function before and above even the fulfillment of their economic demands. In survey after survey, the major demands of industrial workers appear as demands for good and close group relationships with their fellow workers, for good relations with their supervisors, for advancement, and above all, for recognition as human beings, for social and prestige satisfactions, for status and function. Wages, while undoubtedly important, rank well down the list.

To handle the dissonance created by the demands to be economical and the need to be human, people have developed the neurotic behavior we call bureau neurosis.

Workers in Human Service Fields Suffer from Bureau-Neurosis.

Human service workers are people who have chosen to work in a field that serves humans; therefore, one would expect our organizations to emphasize humanity. Surprisingly, this is not the case. Human service workers, like others in society, have the closed world view that bureaucracy is the only way to structure our means of delivering services. This view has become a deeply implanted mind-set that prevents us from looking at alternatives. While tasks may have become more complex since Taylor's pig-iron study, Henry Ford's vision of the assembly line has become "the way" to organize work, even in human services. Food Stamp workers spend days filling out the same forms and using defined guidelines to determine which families qualify for reductions in food costs.

A social worker can leave an agency knowing that in a few days his/her replacement will be able to license foster homes using the specific tests of a "good" foster home that were developed by a committee (a committee which often does not include a foster parent or a placement worker). The task that in reality can have a permanent effect on the life of a child becomes a repetitious job of filling out tedious forms.

We are also faced with the mandate to be cost-effective, but we have not yet found a way to measure the quality of serving people that makes cost/benefits analysis reflective of the social work value system. Nevertheless, there seems to be a human need to produce quality work. Studs Terkel repeatedly reported the dilemma of workers who see no value in what they have produced. He also interviewed the stone mason who did see the beauty of his work--work that would still be standing long after the man had died.[12] The same theme runs through E.E. LeMasters' study of the blue collar aristocrats who take pride in the quality of their work, but who feel defeated with the emphasis on speed over durability when they work on large contracts.

> "You take those apartments we're working on now. There's
> 120 units, almost exactly alike...The goddam foreman
> doesn't care how well we do the job--he wants volume.
> He has orders to complete so many units this week and
> by God that's what he does, whether the work is done
> right or not...I don't enjoy the work any more.[13]

This same cancer--a cancer of quantity and measurable economic indicators, has spread into human services. The intuition and judgement of the seasoned social worker are not valued in a system that measures effectiveness in terms of numbers of people served and cost of service delivery.

We often are left to conclude that one reason the measures of our success focus on economic variables is that society doesn't value what we do. Social workers are lumped together with policemen as the "dirty workers" of society--the segment of the work force relegated to keeping the unsightly out of sight. We dirty workers seem to share the stigma that burdens those who most need release from burdens. We struggle to help others, and for our efforts we sense ridicule from a sophisticated society still wedded to Social Darwinism, still believing that those who need help are innately inferior and that those who help others are in fact upsetting the natural order of things. It is hardly surprising that universities are skeptical of the curriculum of schools of social work, but hold in high esteem the schools of law and medicine.

Within service institutions the anxieties created by bureau neurosis are passed on to the people we purport to help. We are frustrated with the seemingly endless flow of directives by memo, and we pass our anxieties on to persons whose needs seem difficult to meet because of the bureaucratic restraints placed on us. Our view of any organization is as closed as the familiar boxes on the organizational chart. Administrators are seen to us to be "on top" and clients "on the bottom"--that is how they fit on the page on which the chart is printed. This image is so frozen on our minds that even those of us in human services can't hear the conflict between our language and our value system.

The demands on us that our performance be cost-effective elevates the record keeping function of our job to a greater prominence than the human service function. We become frustrated with clients who do not provide us with the information that would contribute to our appearing efficient. At the same time, we ourselves experience an emotional pain that is part of operating in a bureaucracy where communications come in the form of a memo that goes to all personnel like us. We want to cry out that there is no one "like me", but such display of neurotic behavior would show all that we are still "hopeless romantics" who do not understand the nature of modern welfare. So, we suppress our frustration and thus compound our feelings of bureau neurosis. Fearful that we will be found out, we seek safety in the protection of the organizational objectives written for the box we occupy. If an error is made anywhere, we can be better protected by the closed parameters of our duties. We don't have to take risks and we can blame the system for our lack of initiative in trying to find alternatives that may indeed improve the life chances of another person.

We are suffering, along with other workers in our society, from the neurosis of the post-industrial society--bureau neurosis.

Chapter I

Notes

1. Erving, Goffman, Asylums (Garden City, New York: Doubleday and Company Inc., 1961).

2. Studs, Terkel, Working (New York: Partheon Boods, 1972), p. 409.

3. John E. Horejsi, Thomas Walz and Patric R. Connolly, Working in Welfare: Survival Through Positive Action (Iowa City, Iowa: University of Iowa, School of Social Work, 1977), pp, 40-41.

4. Robin Williams, American Society (New York: Alfred A. Knopf, 1960), pp. 454-56.

5. Daniel Bell, The Coming of Post-Industrial Society (New York: Basic Books, Inc. m 1976).

6. Peter F. Drucker, The New Society (New York: Harper and Row, 1962), p.22.

7. Frederick W. Taylor, "Time Study, Piece Work, and the First-Class Man," Classics in Management, Ed. American Management Association (New York: American Management Association, 1960), pp. 67-76.

8. Douglas M. McGregor, "The Human Side of Enterprise," Readings in Personnel Management, Eds. Herbert J. Chruden and Arthus W. Sherman, Jr. (Cincinnati: South Western Publishing Company, 1966), pp. 159-169.

9. Robert Townsend, Up the Organization. (Greenwich, Conn.: Fawcett Publications, Inc., 1970).

10. Bell.

11. Drucker, pp. 47-48.

12. Terkel, p. xvii.

13. E.E. LeMasters, Blue Collar Aristocrats (Madison, Wisconsin: The University of Wisconsin Press, 1975), p. 34.

Peace of mind produces right values, right values produce
right thoughts, right thoughts produce right actions,
and right actions produce work which will be a material
reflection for others to see of the serenity at the
center of it all.

     Robert Persig - <u>Zen</u> <u>and</u> <u>the</u> <u>Art</u> <u>of</u> <u>Motorcyle</u>
                       <u>Maintenance</u>

CHAPTER II

ZEN AND THE ART OF RUNNING HUMAN SERVICE ORGANIZATIONS

Peace of mind isn't at all superficial...It's the whole
thing. That which produces it is good maintenance; that
which disturbs it is poor maintenance. What we call
workability of the machine is just an objectification
of this peace of mind. The ultimate test's always your
own serenity. If you don't have this when you start
and maintain it while you're working, you're likely to
build your personal problems right into the machine itself...
The test of the machine is the satisfaction it gives
you. There isn't any other test. If it disturbs you,
it's wrong...

-Robert Pirsig

Bureaucracy is the machine we use to carry out the complex

tasks of contemporary human service organizations. And bureaucracy

can work. It is not necessary to tie up our clients in unnecessary

"red tape". It is not necessary to crush the enthusiasm of new

workers coming into the agency. It is not ncessary to ignore

the insights of older professionals. Nor is it necessary to immobilize

an agency with fear that is generated by the uncertainty of how

one's success as a human service worker will look when it is converted

into statistics that measure the cost-effectiveness of serving

human beings. Bureaucracy is a machine, a mechanism for doing

what people need to have done. It is the creation of the human

mind and can be controlled by humans. Using Pirsig's metaphor

in Zen and the Art of Motorcycle Maintenance, bureaucracy is a

machine that must be maintained in such a way that it leads to

peace of mind, not to bureau neurosis.[1]

Bureau neurosis is not inevitable; there can be the rationality of bureaucracy co-existing with a component that recognizes the humanness of the people in the organization. We call this other component "humanocracy". We concur with Pirsig's thesis that both the so-called "scientific" and "romantic" perceptions of reality are necessary components if one is to get the most from the machine (in our case, the workings of the human service organization). While the rationality of the scientific mind appears initially to be in conflict with the emotional motives of workers, these two elements in fact are complementary. To repeat Pirsig, "If the machine produces tranquility, it's right. If it disturbs you, it's wrong.." If workers in human service organizations become frustrated and anxious, exhibiting the symptoms of bureau neurosis, the machinery of the carefully defined bureaucracy begins to break down. There are solutions, but only if one frees his/her thinking and accepts as working principles certain assumptions of humanocracy, assumptions that one already knows are true about behavior.

1. Organizations exist to serve the social, as well as the economic, needs of those who participate in them. The work organization provides both the opportunity for direct social contact on site and serves also as a common factor in an individual's existence which can be used to form social relationships after hours. To convince oneself of the strength of this assumption, one could simply do the following:

a. Dispense with all conversations at work that are not directly task-related. This would include the brief rituals of, "Good morning," "How was your weekend?", "I like your new haircut," "That was a good job you did on the presentation Thursday." Of course, the experiment would also necessitate your ignoring all good mornings, compliments, recognition of your children's existence or success, and all the et ceteras directed to you.

b. Do not establish friendships with others in the organization. If you already have friends in the organization, redefine the relationship, and never again use the organization as a place where you meet and get to know people well enough that you allow them to see your humanity. Relate to people in the organization only according to their job descriptions and how these jobs interface with yours.

c. Ignore the absence of others who miss work. Never say, "we missed you yesterday," "hope you are feeling better" and expect the same lack of interest in your existence from others. The only thing that matters is the role; who performs the tasks is irrelevant.

d. Relate to the job definition. If you supervise a family counselor whose job description says that the role occupant will spend one hour a week with each family, buzz the worker's office if she allows a family to stay any longer than one hour. If your job requires that clients complete all intake information before going into your office, refuse to see anyone who does not complete the forms in the allotted time. If agency contract says that a person may have time off to attend the funeral of a parent, grandparent, sibling, or child--be sure that none of your workers go to the funeral of a close friend on agency time.

These are only a few suggestions for insuring that your organization will meet only the economic needs of the people who work with you; but this list probably is sufficient to convince you that organizations do take our social needs into account. "Humanocracy" simply builds on what already occurs informally in the work place.

2. Organizations are a principal (though not an exclusive) context within which life-long human development occurs for people. Human development is going to occur within organizations. It is a basic premise of human psychology that we change continuously from birth to death. Given the existence of this phenomenon, it would follow that this change will occur within organizations, where we spend most of our walking hours. While working in bureaucratic organizations, we do not cease to assimilate information, respond to our social and physical environment, experience a variety of emotions, and adapt our behavior to reduce dissonance within ourselves. We join organizations both because the organization can fulfill certain needs and because we have skills that fulfill the needs of the organizations. This symbiotic relationship further ensures that change in our behavior, our feelings, and our perceptions of life will occur within the organization.

3. The conception, structure, modus operandi and social milieu of the organization influences the quality of human development that its participants experience. Not only will we develop in organizations, but the nature of the organization will directly affect the nature

of that development. In Chapter I, it was argued that rigid

bureaucratic organizations that try to ignore the emotional side

of human behavior are contributing to our development in such a way

as to make us neurotic. Just as Pirsig's unstable cyclist is likely

to build personal problems into the machine itself, the unhappy human

services worker will lack the personal strength to help others.

The pain of the welfare mother may go unheard of by the worker under

fire for not having case recording up to date. The pleas of low

income elderly for adequate homemaker services will be threatening

to the administrator whose cost-effective rating was published as

below average compared with other administrators in the state. The

appeal of foster parents for funding to allow the foster child to

participate in Boy Scouts with their natural child will sound trite

to the worker who fears that his own job will soon be phased out.

These anxious workers will respond to those situations, but it is

doubtful that the response will promote greater self-actualization

in either client or worker.

Again, the conflict described by Bell between the economizing

principle and self-actualizing principle leads to frustration for

the individual. The worker who feels peer support can be open with

other workers and reveal her problems with a family, thus opening

up the possibility of help from fresh insights. With emotional support

and guidance, human growth will occur in the work setting and the

services of the organization will improve. If we recognize that
we do have control of the quality of life in organizations, we can
make changes which allow people to develop in positive ways.

4. A theory of the administration of organizations should,
therefore, include recognition of the importance of human development as a legitimate organizational goal. Recognition of the relationship between worker morale and job performance is not new. Mounds
of data have been collected, analyzed, and published in management
text books. The problem we see with the approaches of these materials
is that they deal with what to do with the consequences of large-
scale, bureaucratic organizations. They do not look at the structure
of the organization itself as the point of intervention. The emphasis
is on working with the individual to help him/her cope effectively
with the status quo so that the person can function in spite of the
dehumanization of the rigid bureaucratic model--not on humanizing
the structure to prevent this demoralization (a part of bureau neurosis).
The goal is to make the worker as productive as possible, not to
create an environment where a human can meet social needs and develop
a positive self-image.

Workers in bureaucracies are human, and they bring their
social and emotional needs to the organization. Administrative theory
may as well recognize the inevitable and deal with human needs in the
structure of bureaucratic management. Handling the consequences of
bureau neurosis is far less time efficient and resource effective.
Working with humans to help them maximize their strengths is more

satisfying to the organization as a whole than is trying to

"rehabilitate" the person suffering from bureau neurosis. One would

do well to prevent the mind-set that justifies employee theft rather

than to prosecute the thief. Since humans are going to develop,

why not allow for an environment where this development can be an

asset to both the individual and the organization?

5. There can be a milieu that facilitates human development,

while not substantially compromising the economic (product) end for

which the organization was formed. In the Western tradition of seeing

reality in terms of dichotomies, administrators and workers alike

have been socialized to believe that we are either rational or

emotional, efficient or inefficient, scientific or romantic. Going

back to Pirsig's allegory, the modern human service agency, like

the motorcycle, can be viewed as a complex machine. The agency

generally operates on the principles of rational organization involving

considerable management investments to assure its continued functioning.

Within the emerging organizational structure both Pirsig's "classicists"

and the "romantics" can be found. The classicists in agencies are

those who aspire to establish a new scientific management system--the

planners, systems analysts, programmers. The romantics, generally,

are found among the social work administrators and line workers whose

professional orientations are more toward the programmatic issues

of the agency.

These two views of running a human service organization often

appear to be in conflict. The scientific management group feels

that by improving administrative control over the organization through

more rational data based planning, only the truly needy will be helped,
and helped only to the extent of their entitlements. The new management
philosophy and approach stresses a need for improved worker accountability and tighter objective measurements of both organizational and
worker performance.

The very nature of human service organizations demands that
we cannot ignore our own humanity. With increasing need for accountability
and avoidance of a waste of resources, we must retain the rational,
bureaucratic model. It is doubtful that without this structure we
could find the tranquility we seek. We join Pirsig's plea for
a reconciliation of this dialectic between rationality and intuition,
for a rapprochement between scientific and romantic perspectives.
It is our position that while the two schools of thought (translated
into administrative approaches) cannot be "integrated", they can
be placed in balance. Reason and intuition are not one and the same,
yet they can be made complementary.

If human service workers are suffering from bureau neurosis
and finding it difficult to meet the needs of the people they serve,
should we not be exploring an alternative model that would prevent
or eliminate the cost of working in bureaucracies while holding
on to most of the benefits. This book proposes an alternative organizational mode, a different mind-set which demands that administrators,
as well as workers, in organizations free themselves of the rigidities
of dichotomies and view the bureaucracy as a total system. There
is no more need to view economic goals as mutually exclusive from

human need goals in an organization than there is to expect a physician to treat a stroke victim without taking into consideration the psychological impact of the patient's paralysis. Our plea is for us to open our thinking to the reality that expecting an organiztion to meet human needs is not new. Organizations have always been influenced by social, as well as economic, variables. Administrative theory should simply recognize the reality of human behavior and provide a framework that allows for the efficiency of bureaucracy and the humanization of humanocracy. Our thesis is:

HUMAN ORGANIZATIONS OUGHT TO MEET HUMAN NEEDS.

A central purpose for which people gather into informal or formal social arrangements is to confirm their social nature. As most philosophers agree, we activate our human qualities largely in the presence of others. Human development is of equal importance to the economic or material reasons for human grouping; when humans organize, they make it so. Administrative theory must recognize this reality.

Human service organizations are designed for several purposes. Clearly, they must produce and deliver a vital product needed by society--a social service and/or an income transfer payment. Thus it should be expected to do so efficiently and effectively. In addition, however, human service institutions deliver services to a highly vulnerable client population and thus must be administered with special consideration to human development as the co-product of the organization. This principle directs that the administrative process and procedures should optimize the quality of human experience for both workers and clients, in balance with reasonable concern for productivity and resource expenditures.

We know that people influence and are influenced by the bureaucratic structure. A theory of humanocracy allows this interaction between intuition and rationality to be more positive and acknowledged-- both for the individual and for the organization. Schumacher argues for accepting this purpose of organizations as being two-fold:

> In any organization, large or small, there must be a certain clarity and orderliness; if things fall into disorder, nothing can be accomplished. Yet orderliness, such, is static and lifeless; so there must also be plenty of elbow-room and scope for breaking through the established order, to do the thing never done before, never anticipated by the guardians of orderliness, the new, predicted and unpredictable outcome of a man's creative idea.[2]

The theory of humanocracy offers a framework by which this totality of purpose can be met. The theory is based on nine principles:

1. <u>Principle of Human Scale</u>. The proposed principle of human scale suggest that there may indeed be a limit to the size of an organization if human development considerations are to be realized. The principle specifies no fixed number of people, but the span of administrative control should be no greater than that in which some reasonable contact between the administrator, worker, and client can take place.

2. <u>Principle of Human Need Satisfaction</u>. Maslow, Fromm, and other humanistic psychologists remind us that all people need a sense of personal identity: respect for their individuality, a positive self-concept, adequate love and support, some reasonable control over their own destiny, opportunity for challenge and a sense of

security. Such ego needs can serve as guides to the ways the administrative process/procedure should be organized and carried out.

3. Principle of Participation. A healthy administrative model requires a broad base of participation in decision-making. At a minimum, those affected by a decision should have some participation in making the decision. If they have a true voice in a decision, selling the change would be unnecessary and enforcement not a problem.

4. Principle of Functional Generalization and Vertical Integration. Contrary to traditional administration theory, humanocracy argues that specialization is not necessarily the key to productivity and efficiency. To generalize means to control a broader range of information and wider set of skills in respect to the agency. It means the capacity to handle a range of assignments and the ability to comprehend the agency system as a whole. The corollary principle of "vertical integration" presents the concept of restructuring organizational arrangements so that people at various levels in the organization take responsibility for some work effort at other levels.

5. Principle of Authority of Merit and Leadership Turnover. Leadership should be earned through both performance and support of those who fall under the pale of leadership. Both upward and downward mobility in organizational life should not only be permitted; it should be encouraged.

6. Principle of Primary Communication. This principle suggests that we communicate on a primary basis whenever possible; and that

we limit the memorandum, case reporting, directives and the like.
Communication on an interpersonal level should govern all relationships:
worker-clients, worker-supervisor, even worker-administrator.

7. <u>Principle of Design Psychology</u>. This principle states that
we should design the work environment to accommodate both work
productivity and human development. A comfortable, attractive,
personalized space in no way should be mimical to getting work done.
On the contrary, by reducing the stresses engendered by the sameness
and sterility of the bureaucratic environment, productivity and
efficiency should increase. A more personal and individualized environment should be good for one's mental state.

8. <u>Principle of Subjectivity and Its Corollaries</u>. A person
is a subject, not an object. While some routinization of policy
and procedure is essential, there must be some freedom to invent,
expand and individualize policy. The organization must have policies
and procedures as guidelines for organizational behavior, but they
should only be guidelines, not prescriptions.

9. <u>Principle of the Convivial Tool</u>. The final principle in
the theory of humanocracy is borrowed from Ivan Illich and his concept
of "the convivial tool."[3] A convivial tool is a policy,
procedure or tool that is so simple that most persons can understand
and use it without the aid of intervention of experts and/or
specialists. Another way of referring to it as a principle would
be to call it the principle of "simplification".

While most of us in human services can adhere to the spirit
of these principles, the difficulty comes in trying to apply them
to the operation of a bureaucratic organization that is overseen
by numerous funding sources that demand accountability. We appreciate
this problem and intend the remainder of this book to describe in
more detail the meaning of these principles in bureaucratic organizations and to outline action steps an administration could take to
supervise an agency that recognizes that meeting human needs is a
vital function of any organization.

Chapter II

Notes

1. Robert M. Pirsig. Zen and the Art of Motorcycle Maintenance
    (Toronto: Bantam Books, 1974), pp. 66-67.

2. E.F. Schumacher, Small is Beautiful, Economics as if People Mattered
    (New York: Harper Colophon Books, 1975) p. 229.

3. Ivan Illich, Tools for Conviviality (New York: Harper and Row,
    Publishers, 1973).

And all work is empty save when there is love;
And when you work with love you bind yourself to
yourself, and to one another, and to God.

Kahlil Gibran - The Prophet

CHAPTER III

PRINCIPLE OF HUMAN SCALE

If it's a small organization, you don't need
...appraisals. Everybody knows everybody.
In a larger company people become pawns. These
big corporations are gonna keep on growing and
the people become less and less. The human
being doesn't count any more. In any large
corporation it's the buck that counts.

Ernest Bradshaw

It was in larger agencies that we in human services first began

to experience bureau neurosis. We followed the pattern of industry

to increase size in order to increase efficiency and to survive in

a world of varied organizations competing for finite resources. But

the corporate model has not served human services well. As agencies

have grown, we have been forced to channel more energy into dealing

with highly specialized departments than in delivering direct services.

A dramatic example of this movement toward largeness in human services

is the restructuring of welfare from a community-based program into

a state system, and now there is a growing trend toward a more

federalized system. In part, it could be argued that these developments

occurred to circumvent the oft times "oppressive" local administration

of welfare. More likely however, such occurrences have developed

to achieve new economies of scale and to improve the management and

control by a central governmental authority. One cannot argue with

the distinct advantage of bureaucracy efficiency. However, the scale of human service organizations is based almost solely on economic and political considerations, not on client need and worker well-being. The price human services have paid for following the lead of business is a high price.

One problem is that bigness has increased vulnerability and potential for disruption. The likelihood of effective management has been reduced as departments have become more specialized and less self sufficient. Delay in delivery of Food Stamps to a family may result from a computer being down. An adult services worker may have to move an elderly woman out of her home and into a nursing home because the homemaker service has already allocated its resources and cannot provide immediate in-home service for this woman. In such super-large systems, the entire organization is at the mercy of its weakest link.

There is also considerable evidence that as any organization grows in size and complexity, it becomes less manageable. The increased inter-dependence of all the parts increases the need for greater control and coordination. We try to achieve this control of the agency by formalizing our appraisals of each other. Our experiences are shared with Ernest Bradshaw[1]: Management is focusing attention on formal evaluation of workers who are little known personalities to the agency directors. "The buck" in human services is increasingly important: we evaluate departments and workers in terms of their cost effectiveness, but we have not learned how to measure care/-effectiveness. Seasoned workers who have been using their reservoir of intuitive skills shaped through years of experience are not being

evaluated on whether or not a family can be helped by their intervention. Success is more likely to be measured by such quantities
as whether or not the family was seen within an allotted time limit.
The worker certifying an elderly woman for Food Stamps is evaluated
by how accurately he/she fills out the application, not by how skill-
fully he deals with a human being going through a painful but necessary
ordeal.

We rely on evaluation instruments that are deceptively "fair".
Following the model used by business, we try to quantify those human
variables that cannot be quantified-compassion, love, concern, empathy,
trust. We reward the vocational rehabilitation counselor who successfully places the most clients; but we forget to ask if the clients
like their job, or if the client will soon be back because the placement
didn't work out. We tend to evaluate the counselor with the clients
who are difficult to place (severely involved cerebral palsy, multiple
orthopaedic handicaps, mentally retarded with severe mental illness,
degenerative diseases, etc.) in terms of numbers that do not adequately
reflect the additional effort his caseload demands.

Another by-product of size is the necessity to communicate by
memo. Information is the blood for survival needed by the bureaucracy.
In written form, information not only is used in decision making
but also "freezes" that decision in time for later examination.
Again, the desired rationality dictated by large-scale bureaucratic
organization conflicts with the human need for individualized conversation. Communication by memo fosters the impersonalization of human
interaction, yet rationality is enhanced. Our minds tell us that

Today we suffer from an almost universal idolatry of
giantism. It is therefore necessary to insist on the virtue
of smallness - where this applies.

E. F. Schumacher - Small is Beautiful

we want to communicate by memo, but emotionally we recoil at the
sight of yet another. "To:...From:...Re:..." lying on the desk. So
long as our organizations are so large and so complex, there seems
little chance of escape from written communication.

It also appears that in large, bureaucratic human service agencies
individual needs and quality of human interactions are relegated to
secondary importance. Public welfare, Social Security, and Medicare-
Medicaid programs can be characterized as large scale, complex, highly
interdependent organizations providing a public service. When similar
services were provided locally and more informally (by county governments, churches, Community Chest angencies, neighbors), there was less
need for regulations to prevent abuse of the system. The helper
either knew the client or knew neighbors of the client. The meaning
of "charity" has been lost from welfare. It is now a huge, uncon-
trollable system devised by people who will never see the people
the system will serve. "Control" replaces caring.

Growth in human services agencies has also injured our public
image (which certainly did not need more negative stereotypes.)
Americans sound like they no longer care about the poor as they consistently attack "welfare", but when a need is perceived, there is
reaction. A family of Boat People is flown directly from the warm
climates of Southeast Asia into a midwestern winter. Suddenly clothing
and blankets appear without requisitions or determination of
eligibility. A garbage man is caught stealing Christmas presents
from the garbage dump for his children and the response to his story
is a cascade of new toys, food, and clothes. It is not charity that

is dead in American; it is the dissatisfaction with a large scale bureaucratic model for administering welfare to people we will never know that brings the outcry from taxpayers.

Another characteristic of large-scale organizations that is both necessary and dehumanizing is the establishment of a rigid hierarchy. Within any large-scale human service bureaucracy, two forms of hierarchy converge. One of these is the superior/subordinate order within the formal structure. The other, more elusive to the casual observer, is the senior/junior informal status based on various factors (sex, race, personal power, etc.). Both of these status systems foster a work climate of repression and alienation, which is exaggerated by the evaluation process. Mandatory formal evaluation converts a supervisor from being a more experienced worker who can offer advice and guidance into an evaluator who will judge us on the scarcity of our mistakes. By appearing confident and competent, we can also increase our personal power and concommittantly our hierarchical position on the informal scale. In a large organization one may find that the mutual support and assistance needed by humans dealing with difficult problems is mitigated against by these systems of hierarchy. The list of problems associated with increased size of organizations seems endless. In addition to the problems already cited, we can turn to an article by Elgin and Bushnell in The Futurist. They described sixteen problems in organizations that are created by bigness alone. Some of those not already covered are:

-Diminishing level of public participation in decision-making.

The cost in time, effort and expense of staying informed enough to participate in the system is substantial and the perceived return from that information is minimal; therefore, a rational response for the individual is to remain passive and ignorant. As a diminishing capacity to participate increases, decision-making becomes more and more the domain of fewer and fewer managers.

-Diminishing capacity of an individual to comprehend the overall system. The units of the system will generally grow in an arithmetic progression, but the inter-relationships between the units will tend to grow in a geometric progression. Therefore, knowledge required to comprehend both the discrete units and their respective inter-relationships tend to outpace the knowledge available to any decision-maker even with the help of computer-based management information system.

-Declining access to decision-makers. As organization scale increases, access by many to the decision-makers becomes diminished. Increased size reduces comprehension, familiarity, and control by the public.

-Growing participation of experts in decision-making. The volume and complexity of necessary information for decision-making processes within a large organization tends to overwhelm individuals. Decision-makers seek assistance from experts, who often have a fragmented, specialized and thus distorted view of reality.

-Dehumanized interactions between people and the system. Rational management practices attempt to de-personalize the system by standardizing human responses within the organization and minimizing human diversity. Conformity, leading to uniformity and predictability, becomes the key value.

-<u>Increasing level of alienation</u>. Expansion of scale increases pervasive feelings of being left out, uninvolved and unappreciated.

-<u>Challenges system values</u>. As a system grows, the sheer number of people and interrelationships will ultimately result in the emergence of a qualitatively different system. The value premises of the original system will become increasingly incompatible with the changing demands of larger systems with more diverse values. Conflict among system members will occur.

-<u>Unexpected and counter-intuitive consequences of policy decisions</u>. As systems become larger, decisions affect more people and more interrelationships, but all people affected do not have enough information to comprehend these decisions. Nor are decision-makers able to assimilate enough information to comprehend the complexity of problems before making policy decisions. The results are oversimplified solutions that have ramifications that could not have been predicted.

-<u>Less innovation</u>. Innovation will tend to constrict as a system grows, because innovation is confined within the boundaries of what the system can assimilate without making fundamental changes. Too many innovations may also be confused as disorder and be perceived as a threat to survival.

-<u>Declining legitimacy of leadership</u>. As a system grows, the system manager has difficulty in both comprehending the total

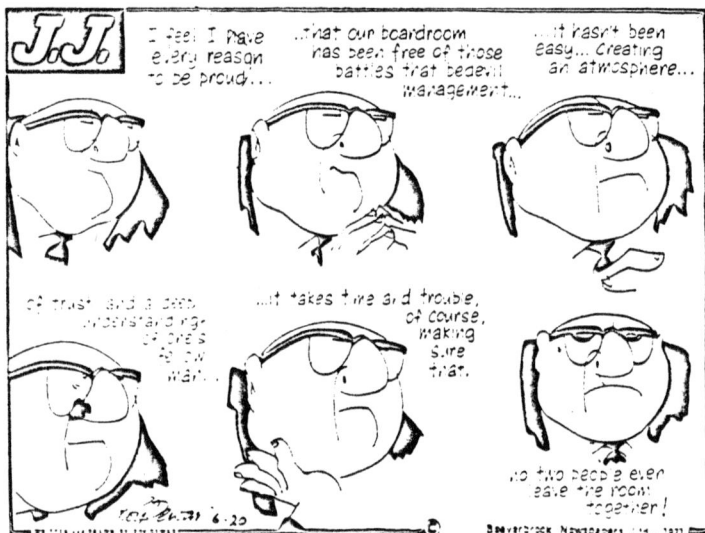

The Washington Post
June 21, 1981

system and maintaining effective contact with his constituency. Consequently, the power to govern drawn from consent of the people is reduced..

-Declining overall performance of the system. If one assumes the validity of the previously stated propositions, one can see that as social systems grow to extremes in scale, the costs of coordination and control will escalate. The comprehensibility of the system will decline, the number and intensity of perturbations will increase, and effectiveness of decision-making will decline.

-Difficulty in seeing the decline of the system. It is difficult to accurately monitor the performance of a massive bureaucracy, establish reliable measures of performance and publicly acknowledge failures of the system. These factors, coupled with the lack of comprehensibility of the system by people, make it difficult to perceive the true extent to which performance is declining[2].

If these criticisms of large-scale organizations are valid, other human service organizations that follow the corporate growth model will tend to decline in performance as they become more complex and increasingly incomprehensible by consumers and funders alike.

Even though there are these obvious disadvantages inherent in large-scale organizational models, we continue to move toward bigness primarily because of the perceived economic advantages: we are convinced that big is better, that a large bureaucracy with the same rules and regulations for all people in a given category is preferable

to a variety of smaller organizations with variable services and
eligibility criteria. Our dilemma is that we have come to a point
where the social costs to organizational members and the advantages
created by the principle of economy of scale represent two divergent
variables within an organization. We have reached the point where
the advantages of increased size are more than offset by increased
social costs.

The proposed principle of human scale suggests that there is
a limit to size of an organization. Likewise, the span of administrative control should be no greater than that in which some reasonable
contact between the administrator, provider and consumer can occur.

Human scale affords the potential for human development, since
it provides opportunity for considerable human interaction on a personal
level. This does not mean that everybody in an organization will
be personal friends or social companions, only that the conditions
ought to be present to facilitate this if desired. An organization
operating under the principle of human scale would likely be comprised
of innumerable small groups characterized by openness, mutual respect,
trust and close inter-personal relations. The groups are ones "...in
which each member must receive an impression or perception of each
other member that is distinct enough to enable the member to react
or give some opinion of each of the others--and to recall later one
or more impressions of each of the others."[3] Although it is difficult
to be definite about the number of members in a work-group". . .five
appears so often in so many environmental situations as to carry
persuasion with it."[4] In analyzing problems of scale, "it is possible

to be almost mystical about the problems of numbers in that some current organizational problems may be traceable to the shift from hunting to agriculture societies many centuries ago, and our social hierarchies seem to date from that shift."[5] It is also of interest to note that, "when people hunted together in bands, their languages seldom had words for numbers over five, which (research)... suggests "is still the most desirable size for an effective small group."[6]

Organization can be broken down into units small enough to take human needs into account. Applied research by the Industrial Democracy Project in Norway and the Tavistock Institute in London have documented this in industries as varied as deep sea coal mines in England, textile mills in Ahmedabad, India, an automobile assembly plant in Kalmar, Italy, and the assembly department of a unionized pharmaceutical plant in southern California. These industries recognize that all organizations are sociotechnical systems and that their organizational objectives can best be met by joint optimization of the technical and social aspects of the system. Human needs are not secondary to production demands, but neither is production disrupted nor limited by a design that recognizes that the workers are humans. And in each instance a key to successful operation is the division of the large unit into smaller, but coordinated, units that meet the criteria of human scale[7]. If such models of organization can be cost/effective for industry, why shouldn't socio-technical design with human scale units be cost/effective for human services. The key to humanocracy may well be in organizing units according to this principle of human scale.

Chapter III

Notes

1. Ernest Bradshaw is the head of the audit department in a bank.
   His observations of work are quoted in Studs Terkel, _Working_
   (New York: Avon, 1972), pp. 521-524.

2. Duane S. Elgin and Robert A. Bushness, "The Limits to Complexity:
   Are Bureaucracies Becoming Unmanageable?" _The Futurist_,
   December 1977.

3. Howard F. Taylor, _Balance in Small Groups_ (New York: Van Nostrand
   Reinhold, 1970), Chapter 1.

4. For example, see Frederick C. Thayer, _An End to Heirarchy:
   An End to Competition!_ _Organizing the Politics and Economics
   of Survival_ (New York: New Viewpoints, 1973), p. 8.

5. IBID, Page 8.

6. Groups of five boys performed more effectively than groups of
   twelve. Mancur Olson, Jr. _The Logic of Collective Action_ (New
   York: Schoclen Books, 1969), Chapter 2. Other evidence can
   be found in Harlan Cleveland, _The Future Executive: A Guide
   for Tomorrow's Managers_ (New York: Harper and Row, 1972).

7. A sample of publications by the members of the Tavistock Institute
   include P.G. Herbst, _Socio-technical Design_ (London: Tavistock
   Publications Limited, 1974); Albert Cherns, "The Principles
   of Sociotechnical Design," _Human Relations_, Volume 29, No. 8,
   1976, pp. 783-792: Frederick Edmund Emery and E.L. Trist, _Towards
   a Social Ecology_ (London: Plenum Press, 1973); and Louis E.
   Davis, Job Design: "Overview and Future Direction", Journal
   of Contemporary Business, Spring 1977, pp. 85-102.

CHAPTER IV

PRINCIPLE OF HUMAN NEEDS SATISFACTION

> Character...is formed primarily by a man's
> work. And work, properly conducted in
> conditions of human dignity and freedom,
> blesses those who do it and equally their
> products.
>
> E. F. Schumacher

If the reader has accepted the assumption argued in Chapter II that human development is a legitimate objective of organizations, we can now look more closely at the second component of humanocracy-- the principle of human needs satisfaction. This principle emphasizes the fact that people demand that organizations meet their human needs - needs for personal development, self actualization, fulfillment and meaning. People are no longer satisfied with putting in their "40 hours", only to pick up a check and then start living. We approach the work-place with a new set of rising expectations. While we might not use Ghandi's spiritual metaphors, we are inclined to share his conviction that work should serve to purify our character. Even Peter Drucker, the hard-nosed organizations analyst, comments:

> Nothing stands out more emphatically in all
> our research than the individual's demand for
> social status and social function. Lack of
> this fulfillment creates profound individual
> and social dissatisfactions, tensions, and
> frustrations, and poisons the entire social
> organizations of the enterprise.[1]

Drucker is not alone in his findings. Emery and Trist similarly
report:

> As society moves from an industrial to a post-
> industrial society, a change in emphasis in
> cultural values occurs. We are moving towards
> the valuing of self-actualization, self-expression,
> interdependence, and capacity for joy over
> the values of achievement, self-control,
> independence and endurance of distress.[2]

Herbst and other members of the Tavistock Institute now vigorously
recommend that we must start adapting technology to meet human needs
in organizations rather than always expecting ourselves to modify
our behaviors to accommodate new technology.[3] Technology originated
to extend the capacity of human senses and energy; it must not be
allowed to obviate the pleasure of these sensate experiences. In
human service organizations where the technologies we rely on are
bureaucratic organization and the computer, we must adapt these aids
to insure that they remain aids, not dictators that contribute to
bureau neurosis.

This need to meet human needs in organizations is compounded
by the change in the family. The further we move from a folk culture
where family members worked together to an urban culture where we
are separated from our families during much of our lives, the more
we rely on the organization to meet many of the needs once met automatically by an extended family. Thus, within formal organizations
workers begin to look beyond economic reimbursement and demands of
work for much of the primariness once reserved for the family. Needs
once met by the family and now brought to the workplace are universal

needs: personal identity, individuality, positive self-concept, affection, security and challenge. Why must we reject the traditional predilection of management to view workers as instruments of production and instead invest in designing organizations that contribute positively towards meeting these needs? Closer examination of each of these human needs helps answer this question.

Identity, The Who Am I of Human Existence.

From birth, we pursue an identity by integrating a personal view of ourselves with the data supplied by those outside of us. In work oriented culture people lean heavily upon work performances and roles for arriving at such a definition. In our society we find that many people are engaged in leisure work, jobs that blend work with leisure. We accomplish the task, we enjoy what this task entails. Leisure work, while designated work, actually gives the same or many of the same rewards as play. The respectability of leisure work reflects the growing desire and even expectation that work should be "fun". In this leisure work world we want our personal attributes to be weighed as heavily as our work role attributes in arriving at a definition of ourselves. We want recognition of not only what we can do, but who we are. This personal self is the hub upon which other components of the self are attached. Unwittingly in the workplace, we often neglect the core itself, while we focus on the culturally ascribed identities.

In human service organizations identity is threatened by labels of "worker", "client", "hyperactive child", "trouble maker", "reactionary", and many others. The labels are inventions of the organizations.

not derivatives of our personalities. These man-made labels in bureaucracies tend to be rigid, narrow and impermeable. They include very little of the material that we consider "personality".

Organizational labels can be positive or negative. They can evidence status and accomplishment or they can be demeaning and a sign of failure. Organization labels simply do not speak to who we really are, a deficiency which humanocracy demands must be rectified. The theory of bureaucracy was designed to reduce personal identity, to fully and totally rationalize our behaviors. Yet, good administration in terms of humanocracy should be predicated on the opposite strategy. Since our sense of personal identity depends so heavily on data outside of us, the organization and its management is in a powerful position to make positive contributions toward defining our total personalities.

There is no mystery to facilitating people's needs for a solid sense of personal identity. In the organizational world we need only to know, respect and respond positively to the attributes of those who are part of the organization. We need to balance our response to people in organizational roles with some responses to them in terms of their personal selves. We could even evaluate how well their personalities contribute to the collective enrichment of those around them, as well as how they make contributions to the economic productivity of the organization.

In organizations where we "know" our workers and clients as people (not labels) we treat them differently, typically more positively. It is not surprising to find that where personal relationship exist, advocacy activities and mutual support are present. The less the awareness of personal qualities of those around us, the easier it is to deal bureaucratically with people as objects, rather than subjects. There is a myth in bureaucratic organizations that impersonal treatment assures equity of treatment. There is little evidence that bureaucracy achieves anything more than equal neglect and/or exploitation of those who fall under its pale.

Much of what we have tried to say about identity can be captured in the following quote:

> That which we have achieved is always in the past, and soon as it is achieved, it is no longer truly related to us. However, that which we have become - our qualities as human beings and our potential for future development - is always in the here and now. After everything else is gone, that which we have become remains, whether we recognize this or not, as the product.
>
> The products of our adult life are rather like a shell that protects the growth of the fruit that is inside. As soon as one realizes that the shell that one has produced is not that which is of essential value, one may discover and make us of what one finds in oneself. However, one can use one's work and one's inner strength to produce no more than an outer shell of success, possessions and pretensions, and then towards the end of one's career one may literally suddenly experience oneself as an empty, burnt-out, and rigid shell, and find that one has gained little of value.[4]

Uniqueness: The Idiosyncracy of Human Existence

Our western scientific mind has led us to study that which is common in people: how we are alike, how we can be fitted into categories of some common genus. Only a few scientists have investigated the phenomena of individual uniqueness. Gordon Allport is one of those few. He was so convinced of the significance of individual uniqueness in human psychology, he created a new concept "proprium" to describe the self.[5] We, too, are convinced of the individual's need to be understood and hopefully appreciated for his/her uniqueness. People who have a personal style are frequently admired for this quality.

Unfortunately, individual style is anthema to a bureaucratic organization. It is generally perceived as a dangerous quality. People with distinct patterns of behavior, that overcome the limitation of the prescriptive behavior, are sometimes viewed as renegades or rebels. The very design of bureaucratic organization and the requisite of prescribing all behavior aims at reducing, if not eliminating, individual tendencies. This fundamental assault on the human personality is seldom recognized by the corporate managers of the larger organizations. They, in fact, pride themselves in organizational arrangements that mitigate independent thinking and maximize compliant behaviors.

It is strange that human service organizations would be inclined to mimic this aspect of the bureaucratic model, given the value our profession places on the principle of individualization. Social workers, in particular, have been trained to appreciate the importance of individualizing their clients; yet, many social workers, upon assuming supervisory and management roles, become troubled by free thinking and spontaneous actions and by those who fail to fit prescribed patterns of behavior.

When offices are look-alikes, methods of service totally standardized, and even agency personnel interchangeable, we know we have failed to implement an administrative model which not only

tolerates, but encourages idiosyncracy within and among its staff.
From the perspective of humanocracy, the excitement of larger organizations rests in the synergetic potential of accommodating and encouraging
differences in worker styles and approaches. Entering a human service
organization should be akin to entering a cosmopolitan community,
a high stimuli experience achieved by building upon worker differences
rather than their similarities. Worker uniqueness is a true asset
in forging a dynamic organization. Each of us has a natural way
of problem solving. When permitted, we get the job done in the best
way possible according to our own skills. With appropriate rewards
for quality performance, we will achieve organizational goals in
our own way without the requirements of heavy handed bureaucratic
controls. (That is, of course, if we honestly believe in the
organizational goals to begin with.)

The fundamental problem of management is to believe that personal
idiosyncracy is a threat to organizational performance. Furthermore,
we must believe that since freedom to be unique is important to human
development, it should be supported within the organization. In
the final analysis making room for individual expression will produce
far greater organizational gains than the traditional practice of
trying to control and standardize invididual worker behavior within
an organization.

Self Concept: The Need for Positive Feedback

The need for positive recognition and approbation is regarded as
another universal need of people, regardless of their social context.

Our needs for positive recognition again go beyond recognition of what we do or how well we do it. We want also to be appreciated for who we are. We want and need positive feedback in both dimensions - doing and being.

In most bureaucratic organizations, there exists a predilection to measure but one aspect of people - task performance (if workers) or compliance (if clients). This tendency results in a feedback pattern that is perceived as negative rather than positive. It has been said that bureaucracies are disposed to recognize only errors of commission, not those of omission. The active doers are more often apt to incur criticism than those who do relatively little. The faceless bureaucrat is not an accident. It is simply an adaptation to the bureaucratic tendency to criticize.

Need for Affection

Love in the workplace is a concept totally absent from the literature of bureaucratic organizational theory and traditional models of management. Perhaps it was because bureaucratic theory was forged during the peak of the Protestant work ethic that reason was the principle variable included in its design.

It would seem reasonable that one of the first steps in the design of our agency administration would be to establish a supportive, affection producing work environment. Management/line relationships, co-worker relationships and worker/client relationships should all evidence a quality of affection. Our relationships with each other should be anything but "impersonal". We need to first acknowledge and respect our basic human worth and dignity before we start interacting with one another from the perspective of our work roles. This, of course, is the first principle of our administrative theory.

There exists a latent fear among many managers that promoting a positive work environment will divert worker attention from assigned tasks. On the contrary, it is only when people do not like each other or distrust each other that they refuse to help each other out or subtly sabotage the work of others.

It would seem that an awareness of the power of sabotage would motivate managers to institute programs to avoid this common consequence of bureau neurosis; yet, there is little evidence that modern management pays much attention to this phenomenon. The organizational theorists developed a strong appreciation for the power of sabotage, but they never were able to make it part of management practice. Instead, the current pool of large organizational managers seems to have placed its hopes on achieving organizational goals in the powers of reason and the modern tools of technology and in the belief that worker compliance (not sabotage) will ultimately be achieved through response to their directives and the threat of dismissal. This manuscript however, questions that a policy of more of the same conditions that lead to sabotage will eliminate it.

But arguing for love to end sabotage is only a persuasive tool to use with the non-believers. To the workers in human services it should appear obvious that love is its own reason for being. It deserves top billing in the workplace, especially where we are delivering human services.

You can fight a man, but you cannot fight the System,
and that is why bureaucracy interposes a System between
you and a man.

Harry Tripper, Jr. - The System and What you
Can Do with It

Security and Active Control Over One's Destiny

Work has tremendous potential for meeting or frustrating these somewhat opposite-type human needs. Survival instincts are strong in humans, and work is the principle medium for economic security and survival in an industrial world. Work also affords a forum for challenging our creative, intellectual and, for some, physical capacities.

Whether the work opportunity contributes in a positive way to meeting these needs depends heavily on the attitudes of management and the policies of the organization. In the traditional bureaucratic approach to management, security is not viewed as being vested in the system, but in the worker's capacity to produce a desired product. Workers are "secure" in their employment as long as they remain competitively productive and the organization continues to experience a viable demand for its services. This stress on the competitive model underlies the bureaucracy's treatment of workers in an instrumental way without reference to them as ends themselves. Many managers feel they have to create artificial conditions of "insecurity" to get the most out of its work force. "Keep them lean and hungry," or so to speak.

It may be true that some workers do increase their productivity out of fear of losing a job or not gaining a promotion. Yet for others, who are basically capable and productive people, the fear and insecurity intimidate them to the point they become less capable of productive involvement. In either case, most workers, when faced with severe competitiveness, find cooperative action very difficult.

They withhold important information for fear another worker would use it to their disadvantage. It seems that it is because of insecurities already present in this world that we create organizations to help us cope with insecurities beyond our control. It is a rather sad statement that we then organize into massive unions to protect minimal levels of income and employment security within these same organizations. The employing agency should assure worker protection as part of its institutional obligations. It would seem that such limited guarantees would motivate worker loyalty and influence worker productivity. The human service agencies have considerable experience with the ugliness that results from human insecurities. They should be the first to design secure and challenging opportunities for their workforce.

There is substantial evidence that much of human history has been written by people in search of reasonable control over their own destinies. For example, political revolutions have basically been produced by persons in pursuit of destroying those forces which wittingly or unwittingly obstruct an individual's freedom of choice. Organizational theory should recognize this human need and provide a base for procedures (both workers and clients) that maximize the control they have on their own futures.

CONCLUSIONS

If we accept the existence of these human needs and the importance of meeting them within the structure of formal organization, the obvious question is "How can decision makers in bureaucratic organizations facilitate the role of the organization to meet human needs

while retaining the components of bureaucracy necessary to meet the

economic goals of the organization?" The answer is a crucial one.

As Schumacher points out:

> In any organization, large or small, there must be a
> certain clarity and orderliness; if things fall into dis-
> order, nothing can be accomplished. Yet, orderlines as
> such is static and lifeless; so there must also be plenty
> of elbow room and scope for breaking through the establish-
> ed order, to do the thing never done before, never anti-
> cipated by the guardian of orderliness, the new, unpredicted
> and unpredictable outcome of a men's creative idea.[7]

The importance of an organizational plan that takes human needs

into account is emphasized in social service agencies, where concern

for human needs is the reason for its existence. As Cherns has

documented in his work, "the process of design must be compatible

with (the organization's) objectives."[8] Pawlak argues that this

goal is realistic: social workers can be trained to "tinker with"

bureaucracy to maximize the possibility of the agency meeting human

needs. While "action steps" for instituting humanocracy will be

discussed in Chapter XII, it would be useful to review here how other

writers have envisioned humanizing organizations to meet human needs:

1. Administrators could solicit criteria for hiring personnel

from individuals in the agency who have a vested interest in how

a person accepting a new position might perform. For example, workers

could draw up criteria to be considered when hiring a new supervisor.

2. Continuing this process, a search committee for new personnel

could include representatives from all levels of the organization.

Increasing input in choosing a supervisor can increase incentive

to work cooperatively with the person chosen.

3. Organizations could allow a range of freedom in interpretation of rules. Experience has taught us all that rules are not frozen and that there is usually more than one interpretation of how a rule can be implemented. An agency could encourage workers to use their own imagination to make rules serve the consumer's needs, rather than allowing the rules to control people.

4. Administrators could encourage white papers that document the need for a policy change. Often those who implement policy can see the flaws in application much better than those who see the policy on paper. On the other hand, one could argue that the line worker does not have the perspective to see the total picture and formulate policy that serves the total organization. Even given this latter condition, we argue that workers can function more effectively as workers and as people if they have some input into the formulation of agency policy. And the additional data can allow administrators to formulate more realistic policy statements.

5. Another suggestion Pawlak makes is that workers be allowed to bypass lines of authority when a proposal is being made. While rational organization has its advantages, the worker needs to know that s/he can control the frustration that results from the sluggishness of papers moving through bureaucratic structures.[9]

Zaleznik's work supports Pawlak: "The main source for the dilemmas leaders face can be found within themselves, in their own inner conflicts."[10] This view of the administrator repeats Chris Argyris and others who seemed to need to tell us the obvious: administrators also have human needs.[11] Administrators cannot be expected to easily organize to meet the human needs of others until their own needs are met.

6. An administrator could try to accept the complexity of his/her own inner conflicts by recognizing that people do have a diversity of motivations. We must handle the more simple conflicts such as wanting a cold beer on a hot day and wanting to stay slim. But we must also deal with conflicting motivations when dealing with a policy decision such as trying to maximize services while minimizing expenses. The administrator who can accept the conflict in motivations can more realistically deal with them. Open discussion of these conflicts can allow the administrator to be more human and also to allow others to deal with these conflicts. It should have the effect of reducing unrealistic demands on the administrator as well. An administrator who can develop a firm sense of identity can share these conflicts with others and thus humanize the environment with her/his openness.[12]

During the twenty-five years that Louis Davis and his colleagues (principally members of the Tavistock Institute in London) have been studying job design on an international basis, they have implemented humanizing changes in a variety of work settings. From the results of their work, one could add to this list of suggestions.

7. One could better find expression of his/her uniqueness in a job situation that allows enough repetition of tasks to provide the organization with efficiency, but still offers enough variety to encourage self-expression. In a welfare agency this might be implemented by allowing an intake worker to occasionally serve on an advisory board. Training of new workers could be rotated among

older workers. Home visits could be mixed with office appointments. The possibilities are endless if an administrator allows the line staff to make suggestions.

8. Davis points to the importance of providing jobs that allow workers to learn on the job. We need feedback from a variety of sources under a variety of situations to continue to deal with the question of identity. In-service training can increase a worker's knowledge and skills, and the use of these skills can add versatility to the staff and flexibility to staff utilization. But once trained, a worker should be allowed to use the new skills.

9. To have some sense of control over one's destiny and be allowed to use one's imagination, a worker must have a body (no matter how few) of decisions which are totally his/her's. Reviewing each case plan written by a worker and occasionally overturning the worker's decisions can be demoralizing and can tell the worker, "I don't trust you." Each worker must have a sense that some decisions can be acted on before waiting for approval from a supervisor. If jobs are filled by merit, job-holders by definition are suited to carry out the responsibilities of the job.

10. Each person in an organization needs positive feedback. Jotting a note to a fellow colleague or picking up the phone and saying, "Good Job," takes little time and says to a person, "You've got support. You're one of us." The disadvantages (real or imagined) of being seen as a brown-noser, politician, or push-over will be outweighed ultimately in the changed atmosphere of the work environment.

There are no data to support the old notion that positive feedback
encourages workers to slough off.

11. The organization needs to provide a person with a sense
that there are means available to meet his/her needs and achieve
one's objectives. Appointment by the buddy system (You're in, so
you get the job) is demoralizing to all. Controlled access to resources
frustrates workers, who need the opportunity to develop new skills.
An agency that allows travel expenses only to top administrators is
blocking other members of the organization from access to important
information. This policy also reminds workers that they are not
important.[13]

In summary, experience has clearly shown that people have needs
that go beyond the job description; that none of us want to be treated
exactly alike, though we appreciate being treated impartially; that
most of us want to experience more than monitoring and performance
reviews; that most of us are afraid of being lost in voluminous regulations and rules over which we have little knowledge or control; that
generally most workers become bored when expected to do the same
thing over and over, day after day; and most workers are distressed
when the future is taken out of our own hands and turned over to
a "management system."

The challenge for the administrator is to establish a work environment and an administrative process that respond to these basic human
needs. Suggestions by other writers on how organizations can address
human needs have been presented in this chapter. In the final chapter
we will present action steps that we feel will help humanize bureaucracy

by taking into account all the principles of humanocracy. A major thrust of this book is a plea for a humanistic approach to management, an approach that recognizes the human needs for individualization, positive self concept, affection, challenge, and security for workers.

Chapter IV

Notes

1. Peter F. Drucker, The New Society (New York: Harper and Row, 1962), p. 49.

2. Frederick Edmund Emery and E.L. Trist, Towards a Social Ecology (London: Plenum Press, 1973), p. 154.

3. P.G. Herbst, Technical Design (London: Tavistock Publications Limited, 1974).

4. IBID., Page 213.

5. Gordon Allport, Becoming (New Haven, Conn.: Yale University Press, 1955).

6. Ivan Illich, Deschooling Society (New York: Harper & Row Publishers 1972).

7. E.F. Schumacher, Small is Beautiful: Economics as if People Mattered (New York: Harper Colophon Books, 1975), p. 229.

8. Albert Cherns, "The Principles of Sociotechnical Design," Human Relations, Volume 29, Number 8, 1976, p. 785.

9. These first five suggestions come from Edward J. Pawlak, "Organizational Tinkering," Social Work, September 1976, pp. 376-380.

10. Abraham Zaleznik, "The Human Dilemmas of Leadership," in Social Work Administration, Harry A. Schatz, Ed., (New York: Council on Social Work Education, 1970), pp. 225-26.

11. Chris Argyris, "Leadership Pattern in the Plant," Readings in Industrial and Business Psychology, Harry W. Karn and B. Von Haller Gilmer, Eds. (New York: McGraw- Hill Book Company, Inc., 1962), pp. 346-66.

12. Zaleznik, pp. 232-33.

13. Louis E. Davis, "Evolving Alternative Organization Designs: Their Sociotechnical Bases," Human Relations, Volume 30, Number 3, 1977, pp. 270-71.

CHAPTER V

PRINCIPLE OF PARTICIPATION

> Manipulative management is producing a society that
> is sluggish, that provides real satisfaction in
> work only to a tiny minority who are somehow exempt
> from management. Manipulation produces tensions of two
> sorts: the discomfort that comes when people feel
> forced every day to be less than they could be, and
> the frustrations we feel when we see the growing gap
> between what we could achieve collectively and what
> we do achieve.

> Richard Cornuelle

Doesn't it appear strange that a society which believes deeply

in political democracy would evolve an organizational model that

operates as a political autocracy? Yet, this is in fact what has

happened. Business, government, even social welfare are built upon

a policy and procedural structure that has had little architectural

input from the "majority". Most business corporations and larger

industrial concerns pride themselves on the "professional"

(ie., exclusive) nature of their decision making.

The large organization industrial model was based on scientific

management and "big boss" decision making. The captains of industry

were "captains" in the purest military sense. They commanded and

the rest followed. In the current post-industrial scene, decision-

making has shifted from boss-made to data-based decision making.

But this is not an actual change. It only means that where there

was once a boss, there is now a unit of decision makers. The captain

now depends for his decision making on the "headquarters" company.

The economist John Kenneth Galbraith calls this group the techno-structure.[1] He argues that organizations have become so large and so complex that it is impossible for any one person to know enough about all aspects of the organization to make top-level decisions alone. The answer has been for these monsterous conglomerates to be governed by groups of people, each of whom is an expert in one aspect of the organization. The skills and knowledge of this techno-structure represent the totality of what was once one "boss". Without the active contributions of each member, the techno-structure suffers just as the "big boss" might suffer if the one part of his brain were damaged. But this techno-structure must rely on secondary information to form a strong basis for decision making. Workers throughout the organization feed information to the data experts. They in turn organize the data and present it to the members of the techno-structure. When the decisions have been made, they are sent back down the lines of the organizational chart and delivered by memo to those who must live with the consequences of the decision. Sometimes the workers even learn of organizational decisions from the press before hearing them from the bosses. Regardless of how workers hear of a decision, for them there remains only compliance.

Human service management is convinced of the efficacy of this functionally specialized approach to decision-making. An "expert" group of data designers, processors and analysts convert agency information into agency decisions with the help of new electronic tools. Workers complain that they are spending more time supplying these analysts with data than providing direct services to clients.

Sooner or later someone's going to catch the imagination
of these people with some new magic. At the bottom of
it will be a promise of regaining the feeling of participation,
the feeling of being needed on earth - hell, dignity.

Kurt Vonnegut - Piano Player

We view with dismay a growing tendency to replace social work types with computer-wise M.B.A.'s and M.P.A.'s in these decision-making positions. This phobic drive for rationality in decision-making is leading to the death of the more humanistic overtones of decisions by human service workers who understood the value of the emotional side of people. Decisions being made in human services seem to be becoming less humanistic. When people are reduced to numbers by an administrator hired for his/her skills in balancing a budget, the human cost of the decision is not computed.

Problems also arise from imposing the conglomerate model onto human services. One is that the needed data must be supplied by the workforce. Without their cooperation the process is subject to severe subversion through passing on bad data. In many human service agencies it is apparent that the line workers, suffering from bureau neurosis, are supplying fabricated data. Unfortunately, if the bad data make the agency look good, nobody seems to care or even notice that a largely illusionary product is being delivered.

People will not be manipulated. If a local office is required to see one hundred clients a month to avoid cuts in staff, the intake worker may record a client contact when someone comes in to ask what time the next eastbound bus stops at this corner. Decision-makers will have their data, but they will not know what the numbers actually represent.

This is the real paradox of data-based decision making strategy: it won't work unless true participatory decision-making arrangements are instituted. Without broad-based worker participation in the decision-making arrangements, workers fail to develop the level of

responsible identification with the organization that is necessary

to encourage them to provide truthful data to measure those variables

we can quantify. More than ever a data-based approach to organizational

decision-making depends upon a functioning democracy within the

organization.

Another problem with data-based decision-making in human services

is that we have not been able to validly quantify our most important

variables. We stumble ahead with a model that seems to be the answer

to accountability. We persist in our belief that we should apply

the cost-benefits model we borrowed from industry, because it works

for them (or so we are led to believe). We are honest. We admit

that we cannot quantify all the variables in human services -- the

ability of a worker to help a client regain a sense of self-worth,

the success of a rehabilitation counselor working with a disabled

veteran to help him re-establish a sense of manhood, the skills of

a social worker in assessing with a displaced homemaker what her

life goals might be. We know we fail at measuring these outcomes,

but persist in fumbling blindly through our borrowed model of data-based

decision-making. We are confident that if we practice

the process long enough, we will find quantitative measures of the

variables the profession accepts as the important ones.

There are other problems with non-participatory decision-making

that go beyond the collection of valid and reliable data. The over-

riding problem is, again, the dehumanization of any authoritarian

model based on scientific management, for as Arnold Tannenbaum
points out:

> Scientific management did not always work - for the
> same reason that the classical approaches to organization
> did not always work. The problem was the human factor -
> that complex, elusive, emotional, social, & sometimes non-
> rational being whose behaviors comprise the substance
> of the organization.[2]

A human being will not be turned into a machine. Russell Baker
in a Sunday Times column, "Murder Most Soul", describes the will
of a desk in its fight to be more than a tool of the industrial machine.
The trouble begins when a young rising "demon memo-writer" stops
going out to lunch and begins eating lunch at his desk to impress
his boss with what a hard worker he is. The desk degenerates:

> The desk had undergone a personality change. Those three
> weeks of being lunched at had given it a glimpse of a
> jollier life. Apparently, it was no happier about being
> a corporate tool than I was, but it had not realized that
> there was a more pleasant side to life until it began to
> serve as dining furniture.

> In this role it was able to provide pleasure and satiety
> to the troubled spirit; it was no longer a brutal
> instrument over which that spirit was stretched as
> upon the rack. The desk wanted to be a dining table.

The writer tried to force the desk to conform to the role dictated
to it by the corporation:

> . . . there was only angry monologue uttered at the
> eloquent silence of this insolent, inanimate quadruped.

> The desk's silences were more eloquent than my monologues.
> "I have the right to be a total piece of furniture," they
> said. "I have the right to hold more than these gritty
> little memos and this squalid out basket and this nagging
> telephone. I have the right to bear steak au poivre and
> hummingbirds' tongues in aspic, to know the sweet weight
> of pork chops, candied yams, Chincoteagues on the half
> shell and chocolate souffles."

You may imagine how difficult it was to get any memos written or enjoy a dynamic romp through the out basket while this infuriating desk filled my head with whinings about lemon meringue pies, baked Alaska, hothouse grapes, roast rack of delicately pink lamb set off with a rare Montrachet, and similar distracting comestibles.

In brief, I yielded to its importunings. Desks have rights, too, as I told the delivery boy when he would arrive bearing roast prime rib of beef, a succulent scallopine of veal or whole roast chickens slowly basted on an open pit. By leaving these great spreads on the desk where I could partake of them throughout the afternoon, I found I could not only satisfy the desk but also get off a few letters and take a phone call or two.

In the end the desk had to be destroyed, shot. It was underminding the morale of all the other desks in the office. Collective bargaining for desks was the next logical step if drastic measures weren't taken.

Bureau neurosis of workers in autocratic organizations often has the same symptoms Russell Baker saw in the desk. Members of a post-industrial society have "tasted" the delicacies of education and have at least vicariously experienced the "good life" through the media. But at the same time, they feel as controlled by the larger society as they are by the bureaucratic organization. They are demanding from organizations the control of their lives that the "American Dream" promises. There have to be some parts of our lives that we can control, and it does not seem to be the larger economic and political order. The dissonance created by the ideal of having control over our lives and the actuality of having no control has generated a new anxiety.

We want peace, jobs, security, honest government, safe streets, etc. However, we experience war, unemployment, insecurity, corruption and threats to self and property. Robert Heilbroner has described

this as the condition of "civilization malaise". There is no longer
a societal connection of "manifest destiny".[3] Neither individually
nor corporately do we feel assured of our futures. We are finding
it almost impossible to make long-range plans. A family saves to
buy a home, then finds that mortgage money is unavailable. A human
services agency becomes aware of unmet needs of elderly people that
force well people to move into nursing homes. The agency develops
services to meet these needs, only to have funding cut two years
later by some unseen decision-makers. The elderly must live (or
die) without the service. The worker who delivers the message never
had any input into the final decision. We live under the uncertainties
and power of inflation, threat of nuclear war, political threats
from countries on the other side of the world, the unpredictability
and irrationality of terrorists, and our first experiences with scarcity
of goods we have always assumed were ours. The wages of workers
in Hong Kong lead to lay-offs of workers in Peoria. The world has
become so complex and inter-dependent that no one group or even nation
has control over its destiny.

Humans will not bend to such oppression. If we cannot control
what happens in India, at least we reason, we will control what happens
to us as we go through our daily routine in Indianapolis. We will
sabotage the organization that tries to deny us the tiny bit of control
over our lives that we still have. As Etzioni points out,

> Leaders who impose tasks on the group are
> more likely to be deposed than leaders who
> direct groups toward tasks the group has chosen.[4]

Bureau neurotic workers have developed a vast repertoire of ways of ridding themselves of these oppressive leaders. Authoritarian decision-makers are daily relearning what should be an axiom: under current conditions, organizational autocracy is doomed to fail. Why, then do we continue to pursue such a collision course? In our continuing efforts to be rational, we have chosen the patterns of authoritarian decision-making that make sense to us because we believe that:

(1) Only those at the top have the information and understand the complexity of the information to make appropriate decisions.

(2) Placing the functional specialization of decision-making into the hands of a few is efficient. The decision-making unit can evaluate each issue and render a decision more quickly than would occur through complex committee processing of a broad based group decision.

(3) The delegation of decision-making to a specific individual or unit helps to assure accountability. The organizational chart can specify who is responsible for a decision and thereby hold them accountable for that decision.

(4) The current model of decision-making produces greater uniformity in decisions. Professional decision-makers, well versed in agency policy, will make disciplined decisions better than a more unweildly body subject to emotions and complex self interests.

Men, by their nature, seemingly, cannot be happy unless
engaged in enterprises that make them feel useful. They
must, therefore, be returned to participation in such
enterprises.

Kurt Vonnegut - Piano Player

(5) Management assumes that its positional status and rewards
    are earned through assuming responsibility for making
    decisions and being accountable for those decisions. Many
    feel they are doing the line workers a favor by freeing
    them of such responsibility.

Current research suggests that the advantages presented by these
arguments do not outweigh the costs.[5] In the first place, the belief
that communication in an organization follows defined lines with
those at the top having all the information available to those under
them is a myth. The location of desks, water coolers, copy machines
and coat racks are as likely to determine who has access to information
as are routing slips attached to materials. Nor should one forget
the ploys of dates, coffee breaks, lunch, etc., as hallowed institutions
for information exchange.

Formal bureaucratic organizations have no systematic way for
dealing with informal organization. The classical theory, in fact,
denies or at least ignores its existence. As morale deteriorates
in an organization, informal organization flourishes. The agency
goes underground so to speak. This is a worker's way of maintaining
some sort of control over his or her destiny.

Nothing brings a work force out into the open like real opportunity
for involvement. The inclinations of people are to provide valid
data when they are also accountable for the decisions produced from
those data. The neat by-product of such an arrangement is that a
participatory decision-making model encourages broad information

sharing. If a person is to have a say in a decision, we will want them to be well informed. Withholding information in such a model hurts oneself.

We also reject the second argument for authoritarian decision-making. Top-down decision making rarely is efficient. An unpopular decision encourages sabotage in the implementation of the policy or procedure. Administrators waste valuable time, energy, and other administrative resources in attempting to monitor and enforce the follow-through intended. It comes as no surprise that modern management has had to invest so heavily in the surveilance of worker activities. This is rarely necessary in a high morale situation.

It has been pointed out that a system of authoritarian decision-making may have been appropriate during the early industrial period when the tasks were onerous and workers uneducated. Today's workers, however, average twelve years of education, and machines have relieved them of many distasteful tasks. Davis states:

> "What is crucial here is not the specific skills that are acquired through an average of twelve years of schooling, but the socialization into expectations and rewards as well as ways of living and working in a school society."[6]

Worker attitudes have shifted from expecting privileges to assuming rights and entitlements. This includes the right to meaningful careers and control over one's work life. On the whole, members of our society are prepared to give control of only a small part of their life space to the organizations for which they work.[7] The response of management to this new reality should not be that of increased policing, but of deepening worker identification with and loyalty to the organization.

One way to increase worker loyalty and accountability, contrary to the fourth argument for authoritarian decision-making, is to adopt a model of group decision-making. The one thing learned from the classic Hawthorne study was that peer groups are the strongest force in enforcement of work rules and regulations. Norman Maier, in his review of the literature on group problem solving, concluded that one of the distinct advantages in involving representatives of people in making the decisions that they ultimately implement, is the time saved in persuading others to abide by the decision. Maier concluded "a low-quality solution that has good acceptance can be more effective than a higher quality solution that lacks acceptance".[8]

A further advantage of group decision-making over top-down decision-making is the pooling of perspectives.[9] Often it is the perspective of a lower ranking employee that provides the insight to produce a creative solution to an existing problem. For example, an intake worker should help decide how to guide applicants through the system. Participation in decision-making broadens his/her understanding, while others have a clearer insight into intake problems.

Our criticism of the fourth argument for authoritarian decision-making is that the assumption of responsibility of the top administrator for all decisions made in the agency gives the small percentage of administrators rewards for all innovative ideas. If a worker has an innovative idea but knows that development of and rewards for the idea will fall to another, why innovate? And if a bureaucratic system "keeps workers in place" by not allowing them to participate in the decisions that will influence their lives, the human spirit

from which innovation flows will be stifled by bureau neurosis.
Participatory decision making encourages each person involved to
be accountable. The authoritarian administrator who thinks s/he
is in control is unaware of how s/he is being manipulated.

Uniform decisions are not an advantage in a post-industrial
society. An open system that allows constant change to adapt to
the environment will help the agency be more in line with the needs
of consumers. A thread of purpose can be expected to run through
the agency because the members, participating in decisions, will
understand the rationale and have a personal commitment to policies
they helped form.

Nor is there any advantage to "uniform enforcement of rules."
The rhetoric alone is dehumanizing. When organizations are limited
in size to human scale, people can be individuals and individual
concerns can be confronted. The false safety of the contract is
replaced by the humanizing atmosphere in which the individual can
belong by being part of governance. As Etzioni points out:

> Not all that enhances rationality reduces happiness,
> and not all that increases happiness reduces
> efficiency . . . Thus, to a degree, organizational
> rationality and human happiness go hand in hand. But
> a point is reached in every organization where happiness
> and efficiency cease to support each other ... Here
> we face a true dilemma.[10]

But, we argue this dilemma can best be handled by allowing mediation
between individual needs and group goals to be conducted by those people
who will most be affected. Bureau neurosis is not caused by our
having to make concessions to the group, but by our feeling of helpless-
ness in not having control over how concessions will be made.

Chapter V

Notes

1. John Kenneth Galbraith, Economics and the Public Purpose
   (Boston: Houghton Mifflin, 1973), pp. 81-91.

2. Arnold S. Tannenbaum, Social Psychology of the Work Organization
   (Belmont, California: Wadsworth Publishing Company, Inc.,
   1966) p. 16.

3. Robert Heilbroner

4. Amitai Etzioni, A Comparative Analysis of Complex Organizations
   (New York: The McMillan Company, 1971), p. 40.

5. Peter M. Blau, Bureaucracy in Modern Society (New York: Random
   House, 1965), Chapter 5.

6. Louis E. Davis, "Evolving Alternative Organization Designs:
   Their Sociotechnical Bases," Human Relations, Volume 30, Number
   3, 1977, p. 264.

7. Page 264

8. Norman R.F. Maier, "Assets and Liabilities in Group Problem
   Solving: The Need for an Integrative Function," Psychological
   Review, 1967, 74:240.

9. Page 240.

10. Etzioni, p. 2.

CHAPTER VI

PRINCIPLES OF FUNCTIONAL GENERALIZATION AND

VERTICAL INTEGRATION

Unless the members of the organization have the
freedom and initiative to deal with operating
problems as they come up, efficiency will suffer.

Peter Blau

In spite of the warnings of Blau and other sociologists, we

have persisted in conceptualizing organizational designs with

specialized roles and vertical hierarchies. Tasks are subdivided

and carried out by different individuals and units located within

the various levels of the organization. Human service organizations

have followed the factory model. As Olmstead argues, "staffing patterns

and task assignments within such organizations should be made on

the basis of the efficient fulfillment of the purpose and function

of the organization."[2] Thus, the intake worker completes the intake,

the protective services worker serves to protect children and the

vocational rehabilitation counselor helps rehabilitate the handicapped

for vocations. The supervisors supervise the workers, and the agency

director represents the agency to the Board. Roles are clearly defined,

specialized, and related to each other according to an organizational

chart.

Human service agencies have adopted this model because we are seeking efficiency and rationality within a system that allocates resources on the basis of both society's goals and the profession's norms. Society's goals for us seem clear: provide a minimum income and the necessary services to convince us that we are humans, but do so in a cost-effective manner that will demand the least sacrifice from the "haves" and the least visability of the "have-nots". We believe that we can meet this charge, and thus be accountable, if we can show that we are organized according to technical competence and a clearly defined division of labor.

These models also mean that individuals with different skills perform different, yet complementary, functions (functional specialization). By segregating the tasks, it is assumed that management can better control the workers. Where tasks are specified, we can trace an error to its source.

While theoretically, at least, functional specialization and vertical hierarchy make sense, there are drawbacks to a devoted adherence to the specifics of these models in human service organization. When a human service program is based on a specific definition of a social problem and is operated by highly trained specialists, the relevancy of program with the real world of service needs is questionable. Human service needs and human service organizations operate at two different rates. It takes time for an organization to gather information required to study a social problem, design a program response, hire and train professionals, and deliver a service.

This temporal difference is also affected by the respective

perspectives of a professional specialist with a trained, but distorted,

view of reality and the persons who are actually experiencing the

impact of a social problem. In other words, "Time to know is different

from time to do." Consequently, a permanent tension exists between

the demand that an organization deal with the world as it is, and

its speed in mobilizing the technical skills and resources required

to appropriately address ever changing problems. This tension is

increased when functional specialization is rigidly adhered to and

followed within the organization. Specialists must be retrained

for another speciality when a "new" problem arises. Another problem

with a close adherence to this model is that it does not recognize

that the "experts" are the people who have experience with a position

and have incorporated their own personal skills and knowledge into

doing a task in a way that is best for them (but not necessarily

best for anyone else). For example, good line workers have the most

client contact and have learned how they deal most effectively with

people needing help. An analyst may come in and do a time study

to determine what percentage of each day the line worker should spend

on each task outlined in a task analysis of the job, but following

this guide may prove even more inefficient. As Blau pointed out:

> ...To repress the ability for self-imposed discipline
> and to undermine the motivation to exert efforts
> by prescribing in detail how every task is to be
> performed is wasteful, to say the least.[3]

The specialist learns more and more about less and less
until, finally, he/she knows everything about nothing;
whereas the generalist learns less and less about more
and more until, finally, he/she knows nothing about
everything.

Donsen's Law

A social researcher may spend years and thousands of dollars breaking down the factors that describe a good foster home, but the outcome will be that this scientifically defined rating will correlate most highly with an experienced social worker's rating. The worker has learned from years of experience to pick up on tiny cues that provide insight into parenting and other skills, which a successful foster parent must have. The worker's skill has become so refined that it may appear to be intuitive, but this simplistic explanation only veils a very complex process that is based on experience. To expect this worker now to assign weights to a long list of characteristics of the foster parents, and then to allow the supervisor to license the home on the basis of the parent's final score, denies the skills of the worker and leads to a more complicated and time-consuming process. (In reality the worker quickly learns how to fill out the form in such a way as to procure licenses for the homes she wants anyway). By specifying specialized tasks (data gathering and decision-making), it now takes two people at least twice as long to accomplish a goal that one more generalized person had performed more quickly.

Not only is specialization more time-consuming and inefficient, but it also is not realistic. Human problems are not easily separated into distinct facets that can be dealt with by one helper now and then with another later. A fifty year-old man who has been laid off work is suffering from hurts that feed on each other - his loss of income, his lowered self-esteem, the disturbance of home life, the confusion about the future - and so on. To define his problems as distinct parts of a machine and then send him down the human services assembly line is what he calls "getting the run around". It's what human service workers call inhumane. The team approach to problem solving that is becoming increasingly popular is more reflective of the holistic nature of human problems. Specialization of tasks moves us farther from reality.

In addition to the time required to produce efficiencies associated with highly specialized people, this time is increased with the high turn-over rates usually found in high-stress human service roles. One of the most talked-about phenomenon in human service administration today is "burn out", or plateauing. Burn out as explained by Dr. Christina Maslach occurs "when your emotional center goes. There is nothing that you really care about. You don't have any optimistic feelings, only negative ones. You don't like the people you work with and wish they would go away. You treat them in institutional, routinized, and dehumanizing ways." For persons assigned to emotionally-charged tasks within human service organizations, burn-out will occur even though professionals strive for a attitude of "detached concern."[4]

Bureaucratic organizations are inherently stress producing. Some of the causes for stress are found in the model's expectations of compliance, coordination, and conformity, and in the impersonal nature of its internal and external relations. Consequently, patterns of rigidity, goal displacement, ritualism, and communication failure within the chain of command all demand varying patterns of personal adjustment. The personal cost of such an adjustment is a serious problem. This problem is compounded when the bureaucratic model is imposed on a human services organization. The very nature of the problems the organization is charged to deal with conflicts with the rationality of specialized role definitions and vertical hierarchies. Maybe the expectation of the agency rules, regulations, and procedures is that external relations are impersonal; however, the reality is that it is people with personal problems with whom we are dealing. Even with specified rules and procedures, we can only deal with each person personally. Is it any wonder that workers in human services experience burn-out? This unrealistic demand that workers separate their personal feelings from their professional roles takes a heavy toll. It not only stifles personal development, but it also can foster problems of alcoholism, marital conflict, and emotional illness. It most certainly will be a major contributor to the development of bureau neurosis.

Another problem with specialized role definitions and hierarchial organization is that only a few people (typically those in the top boxes of the organizational chart) comprehend the totality of the system, its full range of rules, regulations, programs, and goals. The other members are expected to carry out the programs on faith that what they're doing somehow complements what everyone else is doing. Taken out of context of the system, few rules and procedures actually do make sense. This lack of understanding may account for the attitude of many workers toward directives that come down from above. Such directives may be received with "what can I do to avoid following through on this?" We see such bureau neurotic behavior as workers saying to clients, "I'm going to ask you this question and your answer,

if you want to receive this service, should be ..." Administrators
who tell themselves that only they have the perspective to make policy
are ignoring the often documented fact that workers can sabotage
any directive if they choose (and they choose). Also, the possibility
of implementation is difficult to measure if you don't consult with
those who will implement.

In addition to these problems associated with specialization,
Davis, from his studies of a variety of work settings, has concluded
that there are also other problems associated with the pyramid structure
and specialization:

1. The concept that ownership carries with it absolute authority
automatically sets up conflict between the owner and the worker.
In human services, we don't "own" anything; the assumption is that
the "taxpayer", "community", "church", or funding source owns us.
If we accept these non-profit funds, we are accepting this machine
status. The top administrators are the mediators with these funding
sources and thus have a clairvoyance that we workers do not share.
The administrators are frustrated that the workers don't like the
rules and procedures; the workers are insulted by the tone of the
memo. A "we/they" situation is set up and the bureau neurotic workers
go underground. The administrators, who have carefully considered
the policy and genuinely believe that it is the best statement possible
see the workers as trouble makers, and they too, become more bureau
neurotic. The final attack comes in the announcement that the workers
have organized and will begin collective bargaining.

2. Another problem with the concept of specialized roles is that the human services worker is not an inanimate tool. Davis points out that the implicit success strategy of classic organizations was based upon, and continues to require, that people become single-skilled, or single-purpose instruments, narrowly self-centered, and immediately responsive to simple rewards. Davis found that this approach to administration led to apathy, hostility, fragmented tasks and services, and overblown bureaucratic superstructures. Bureau neurotic workers are not going to perform as well as happy workers; they will require more administrators to push them along. And all these administrators must be coordinated -- and so the organization grows.

3. Davis also believes that when we define what needs to be done and how it is to be done only by logical and scientific means, we are again being grossly unrealistic. Organizations that operate under this assumption are so structured that line workers are the spare parts and the staff specialists are the repository of learning from organizational experience, with a consequent loss of talent from the workers and a loss of organizational learning from the administrators. He goes on to say:

> The fractionation of tasks required, and continues to require, an organizational superstructure of many layers to both cement together the disjointed pieces and deal with the internal and external disturbances that arise. The needs, abilities, aspirations, and ideals of society brought by individuals into the work place have served as a constant and growing source of difficulty, irritation, disaffection, and malfunction in classically structured organizations based on the bureaucratic-scientific management assumptions...[5]

We in human services might listen to Davis and question whether the increase in size of our service organizations is due solely to expanding our services, or if we have grown simply to accommodate the layers of bureaucratic management necessary to control bureau neurotic workers. The answer certainly is not so simple as the question implies. The principles of functional generalization and vertical integration are designed to combat the social costs described above.

To generalize necessarily means to control a broader range of information and a wider set of skills relevant to the organization. One has the capacity to handle a range of assignments and to comprehend the organization as a whole. Blau sees functional generalization to be a component of the bureaucratic model:

> Bureaucracy, then, can be defined as organization which maximizes efficiency in administration, whatever its formal characteristics, or as an institutionalized method of organizing social conduct in the interest of administrative efficiency. On the basis of this definition, the problem of central concern is the expeditious removal of the obstacles to efficient operations which recurrently arise. This cannot be accomplished by a preconceived system of rigid procedures, as the preceding discussion suggests, but only by creating conditions favorable to continuous adjustive development in the organization. To establish such a pattern of self-adjustment in a bureaucracy, conditions must prevail that encourage its members to cope with emergent problems and to find the best method for producing specified results on their own initiative, and that obviate the need for unofficial practices which thwart the objectives of the organization, such as restriction of output.[6]

Vertical integration replaces the concept of power as a function of placement in the organization. The base of power is shifted from coercion and threat to more reliance on reason, collaboration and

17

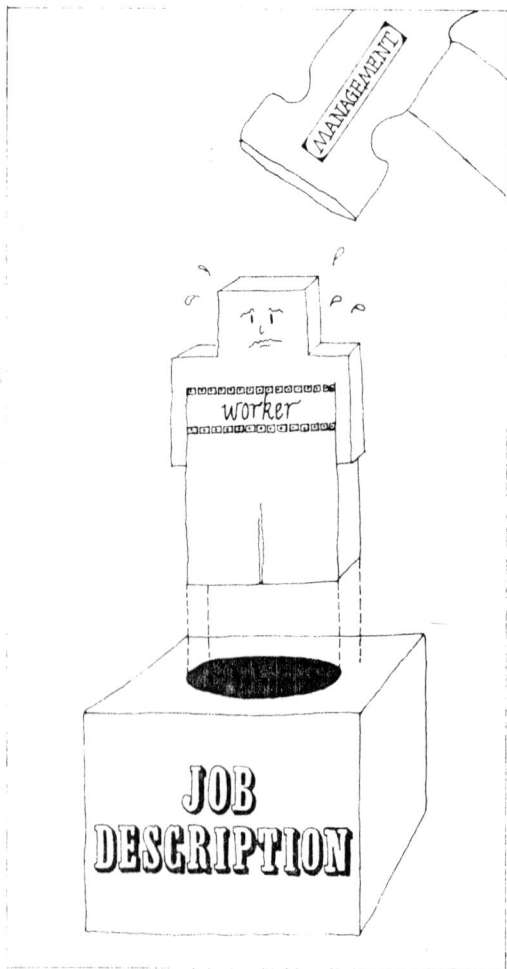

if you want to receive this service, should be ..." Administrators

who tell themselves that only they have the perspective to make policy

are ignoring the often documented fact that workers can sabotage

any directive if they choose (and they choose). Also, the possibility

of implementation is difficult to measure if you don't consult with

those who will implement.

In addition to these problems associated with specialization,

Davis, from his studies of a variety of work settings, has concluded

that there are also other problems associated with the pyramid structure

and specialization:

1. The concept that ownership carries with it absolute authority

automatically sets up conflict between the owner and the worker.

In human services, we don't "own" anything; the assumption is that

the "taxpayer", "community", "church", or funding source owns us.

If we accept these non-profit funds, we are accepting this machine

status. The top administrators are the mediators with these funding

sources and thus have a clairvoyance that we workers do not share.

The administrators are frustrated that the workers don't like the

rules and procedures; the workers are insulted by the tone of the

memo. A "we/they" situation is set up and the bureau neurotic workers

go underground. The administrators, who have carefully considered

the policy and genuinely believe that it is the best statement possible

see the workers as trouble makers, and they too, become more bureau

neurotic. The final attack comes in the announcement that the workers

have organized and will begin collective bargaining.

2. Another problem with the concept of specialized roles is that the human services worker is not an inanimate tool. Davis points out that the implicit success strategy of classic organizations was based upon, and continues to require, that people become single-skilled, or single-purpose instruments, narrowly self-centered, and immediately responsive to simple rewards. Davis found that this approach to administration led to apathy, hostility, fragmented tasks and services, and overblown bureaucratic superstructures. Bureau neurotic workers are not going to perform as well as happy workers; they will require more administrators to push them along. And all these administrators must be coordinated -- and so the organization grows.

3. Davis also believes that when we define what needs to be done and how it is to be done only by logical and scientific means, we are again being grossly unrealistic. Organizations that operate under this assumption are so structured that line workers are the spare parts and the staff specialists are the repository of learning from organizational experience, with a consequent loss of talent from the workers and a loss of organizational learning from the administrators. He goes on to say:

> The fractionation of tasks required, and continues to require, an organizational superstructure of many layers to both cement together the disjointed pieces and deal with the internal and external disturbances that arise. The needs, abilities, aspirations, and ideals of society brought by individuals into the work place have served as a constant and growing source of difficulty, irritation, disaffection, and malfunction in classically structured organizations based on the bureaucratic-scientific management assumptions...[5]

compromise. This view replaces an ever simplified push-button view of workers and presents the idea of organizational arrangements so that people at various levels in organizational hierarchy take responsibility for some work effort at other levels. Administrators would never be "pure" administrators, line workers would not be the only ones seeing clients, and secretaries would not find themselves alone doing the typing and filing. Movement toward the use of teams in human services has shown that successful teamwork holds much potential for both accommodating organizational needs and helping clients meet individual social development needs.

One advantage of generalized job descriptions is that it encourages creativity as Schumacher notes:

> Experience shows that when we are dealing with large
> numbers of people many aspects of their behavior
> are indeed predictable; for out of a large number,
> at any one time, only a tiny minority are using their
> power of freedom, and they often do not significantly
> affect the total outcome. Yet all really important
> innovations and changes normally start from tiny
> minorities of people who do use their creative freedom.[7]

Redesigning jobs around these concepts of functional generalization and vertical integration enables individuals to recharge emotionally. Shifting assignments to change the amount of face-to-face work with clients, engaging in short term administrative tasks, varying the type of client problems seen or the modality required and reducing the volume of clients to be served are examples of ways to combat emotional burn-out. While a primary assignment would be necessary to provide stability to work flow in the organization, and to maintain organizational cohesion, the opportunity to "cross over" and to move

up and down in the work hierarchy has tremendous psychological
advantages to individuals who feel "trapped", bored and alienated
by the organization. Motivation studies have documented that opportunities for personal growth and for recognition in the organization
are much stronger motivators than is money. A worker who feels that
the organization knows and appreciates him or her will be a loyal
worker.

One alternative to vertical hierarchy is compartmentalizing,
the placing of professionals in units composed of mainly their peers.
This allows an organization to develop what Etzioni calls a "concomitant
division of compliance". Concomitant divisions of compliance are
structures operating in different subunits of the same organization
concurrently but independently.[8] Such divisions are especially useful
in organizations needing different professional orientations. They
allow compliance with a low degree of alienation.

Compartmentalization requires less reliance on final rules,
paper flow, and other bureaucratic elements which tend to increase
work stress. Formalization can be limited to broad, established
policies and regulations necessary for efficiency. Compartmentalization
can serve to reduce the number of hierarchical levels through which
communication must flow between management and workers. Not only will
blockage and distortion be reduced, but conflict resolution and problem
solving can occur in a more timely fashion. The general decentraliza-
tion of decision-making caused by compartmentalization allows increased
participation by all persons in a relevant fashion. Such team
approaches also represent meaningful support systems for individuals.

Another important advantage of functional generalization and
vertical integration is that a more holistic view of the agency and
its goals is possible when people can move among roles and assume
initiative in problem solving. Workers have the opportunity to understand the functional relationships between tasks within the organization. This provides a basis on which mutual appreciation and respect
of the functional interdependence of all persons within the organization can be established. The rationale behind rules seems clearer
and organizational sabotage ceases to make sense. People know each
other and understand better how the organization operates. There
is less need for authoritarian administrators to develop procedures
to control workers. The structure of the agency can be simplified.
In short, the structure that appears on paper to be so efficient
is not efficient. The structure of humanocracy that takes into account
the power of the human spirit is ultimately the more efficient and
rational organizational structure.

Chapter VI

Notes

1. Peter M. Blau, Bureaucracy in Modern Society (New York: Random House, 1965).

2. C.B. Olmstead, "Some Management Principles of Staffing Social Welfare Organizations," Social Work, Vol. 6, No. 3, July 1961 p. 22.

3. Blau, p. 60.

4. Christina Maslach, "Burn Out, A High Price for Caring", The National Observer, July 11, 1977, p. 14.

5. Louis E. Davis, "Evolving Alternative Organization Designs: Their Sociotechnical Bases", Human Relations, Volume 30, Number 3, 1977, pp. 262-63.

6. Blau, p. 60.

7. E.F. Schumacher, Small is Beautiful. Economics as if People Mattered, (New York: Harper Colophon Books, 1975) p. 217.

8. Amitai Etzioni, A Comparative Analysis of Comples Organizations (New York: Free Press, 1964), p. 266.

CHAPTER VII

PRINCIPLE OF THE AUTHORITY OF MERIT AND LEADERSHIP TURNOVER

> In a hierarchy every employee
> tends to rise to his level of
> incompetence.
>
> Dr. Lawrence J. Peter

Since the publication of the Peter Principle in 1969, we have all been aware of the fact that in many large bureaucracies workers tend to rise to their level of incompetence. The "Peter Principle" operates because people can move up the bureaucratic structure by evidencing competent performance in a lower position and then staying in the organization long enough to be promoted. The key is not so much talent, as endurance. The Peter Principle might well be called the "Seniority Principle" in many cases.[1]

One may not have to stay in the organization long enough simply for a position to open. A competent worker may be promoted to become an incompetent administrator. How many master teachers have become ineffective principals? Insightful and imaginative social workers are promoted to administrative positions demanding skills in budgeting and policy making, skills they don't have and aren't interested in developing. We look at hierarchies and impose the model that "higher up" is more of whatever makes up "lower down". We know this is not the case, but we move people through the hierarchy as if it were.

Different jobs take different skills. Being successful at one job does not guarantee that we will be equally successful at another job; nevertheless, when a position opens, we look at a person's success in another job. We seem to forget to analyze the skills that led to this success and question whether or not those are the competencies the new position demands.

Even in those instances where it is true talent that enables a person to climb the hierarchial ladder (merit), it is not infrequent to find the person shifting from basing authority on merit to basing authority on position. The hungry, untenured young instructor, actively researching and writing, often becomes the fat and lazy tenured professor producing only enough to hang on. Once tenured, the person who relies on the authority of position becomes almost impossible to dislodge. Society encourages this transition. When a person receives an M.D. degree, we quote him/her as an authority on everything from human sexuality to world politics - neither of which s/he knows much about since his/her medical studies occupied most of his/her attention for ten years. When the college president walks down the hall, faculty and students alike stand in awe. The Dean of the School of Social Work is "Dr. _____"; the student is "John".

Just as the line worker's identity is depersonalized in routine tasks, the administrator is engulfed in a role - a role with such assumed grandness that we forget that there is a human being in the position. We are astounded if she errs, we are incredulous if he becomes depressed. The person who moves to a higher position in the hierarchy is given no more room to be human than is the line worker.

The Big Nurse tends to get real put out if something
keeps her outfit from running like a smooth, accurate,
precision-made machine. The slightest thing messy or
out of kilter or in the way ties her into a little white
knot of tight-smiled fury ... I know, I can feel it.
And she don't relax a hair till she gets the nuisance
attended to - what she calls "adjusted to surroundings."

   Ken Kesey - One Flew Over the Cuckoo's Nest

Is it not logical that s/he begins to believe that s/he is one with the position? S/he knows s/he can err (and thus not seem to merit the position). A person's security may begin to come from the authority of the position, not the authority of the less dependable merit.

Whatever the explanation of why individuals come to rely on the authority of their organizational position, we can observe that they do. This is historically expected behavior. Since the implementation of the bureaucratic model, authority of position has been seen as essential to the functioning of the large bureaucracy. Blind obedience to authority was believed to be imperative to efficiency and to controlled management. It was the position, carefully delineated, with clear protocols of worker behavior that was the cornerstone of modern bureaucracy. Not having to deal with subjective differences and uncertainty was to be the basis for eliminating controversy and insuring conformity.

But workers are not machines. They do not follow the lead of an incompetent person; nor do they remain hidden, let alone contained in their positions. Their personalities spill over the bounds of performance; they contribute to the agency milieu. Their attitudes and enthusiasm (or lack of) affect the total work environment. The Civil Rights Movement of the 1960's and the "Me" psychology of the 1970's, can be seen as examples of societal ramifications of rationality's attempt to stifle our emotional growth. If an incompetent leader relies on authority of position, workers will look elsewhere for leadership.

This phenomenon can be understood if one accepts as a definition that leadership is the phenomenon of activating the energies of others by not only doing what is expected, but doing it in a "way" that stimulates the performance of others up and down the line. In these terms anyone and everyone can be a leader. Leadership is energizing others, not occupying a position that carries the label "leader".

Anyone who has been involved with organizations for any length of time realizes that the energies in an organization (like opinion leaders in the community) can come from the most unexpected people. Frequently, it is the charisma of a receptionist or the concern of a caring board member that "moves" a human service organization by stimulating agency energies. We (the authors) were once associated with an organization where a mentally retarded man (assigned to care for a small coffee shop) was a core energizer of the workers in that setting. His positive attitude, humble ways, and compassion for human suffering moved all of us to react in similar ways.

If, then, we do not subscribe to the traditional principle of authority of position but, rather, believe that leadership can come from anywhere in the organization, how do we propose to establish recognized authority positions? Our alternative principle -- the authority of merit -- simply suggests that each person in a position of authority should remain in that position only as long as s/he continues to merit the position. The principle is based on the most basic of realities, namely, that we only have real power if others agree to accept our authority. Since social power is power "over" others, power must ultimately be determined by these others.

Thus, the principle of authority of merit insists that one's authority be defined and measured by those people who will be most moved by this authority. Usually, this will be people in immediately superior positions, those equal to people slightly inferior in rank, plus those ultimately affected by the service, the clients of the agency or the professor's students.

In traditional agencies employees tend to be evaluated exclusively by superiors. Even in universities, tenure decisions are often limited to persons equal to or above in rank. (Fortunately, the professional evaluations increasingly include student evaluations of their professors.)

The higher-in-rank evaluation model reinforces the bureaucratic notion that authority rests within positions themselves: only superiors are competent to evaluate performance. The alternative principle postulates that we cannot know whether a person really merits a position unless we have substantial evidence from people under as well as over, the person being evaluated. To know that a person is "able" to do a job (as measured by a merit examination) is not the same as actually doing that job. In leadership positions, doing a job is often getting other people to do their jobs. However, how can we really know whether others are doing their jobs without input from those being supervised?

This is not a new concept. In some religious denominations there is a very simple procedure for selecting a pastor. The congregation meets, votes and "calls" the minister to the position.

The congregation regularly affords a vote of confidence (gives evidence that the pastor continues to merit his calling). Many democracies, likewise, have protocols for critical votes of confidence when leaders appear to lose their following during their periods of office. It is this type of authority model that we feel should characterize the human service organization. If followed, the agency can be assured that its administration always has the confidence of its staff (and hopefully of the clients).

Admittedly, there are limits to the principle of the authority of merit. Votes of confidence are not to be capricious acts. Leaders must be given full opportunity to "earn" merit (not to be confused with popularity). The competencies expected of the position must be clearly defined to avoid an assessment of personality. Evaluators must also be able to respond to characteristics without feeling that they are involved in an assault on a person's character. Every effort must be taken to preserve as much objectivity as possible.

Time is another essential variable. New workers are given a probationary period; new administrators should be expected to live by these same rules. It takes time for a person to learn a job and to develop the relationships necessary to motivate workers to follow leadership. People are cautious about allowing someone to have power over them. A premature evaluation might be a reflection of an unexpected honeymoon period or of insufficient time for a leader to win worker trust.

In keeping with the same goal of assuring vital leadership in the human service agency, we also assert the necessity of leadership turnover.

In any organization, the potential is much greater for
the subordinate to manage his/her supervisor than for
the supervisor to manage his/her subordinate.

Rodouic's Rule

Workers bring the same, tired problems. You get tired of fighting the same obstinate battles. Some workers seem determined to undermine whatever you propose, no matter how hard you try. You become discouraged and tired of fighting dragons. You start hearing yourself say, "We tried that and it didn't work" instead of "That's a good idea" or "Maybe it will work this time." Administrators are as vulnerable to bureau neurosis as are workers.

Perhaps the most important aspect of leadership turnover is that it allows the administrative group to be recycled, to re-experience other roles and functions in the agency. An agency is tightest and experience is greatest when the workforce appreciates the role of all co-workers and remains closely connected to the client group being served. By moving people around to insure that they at least occupy their level of incompetence a minimum length of time, we are also instituting a system by which people learn several roles and thus can be more versatile -- the goal of the principle of functional generalization discussed in Chapter VI.

Thus we advocate that some reasonable limits be placed on the terms of office of anyone in a leadership position. Even in cases where an administrator is performing at a high level, some reasonable rotation should take place. This would allow others aspiring to leadership positions to be assured of the opportunity (if merited). It further permits those who are barely meeting the demands of the administrative position to leave without losing face. By implementing the complementary principles of authority of merit and leadership turnover, we have created both the possibility of "impeachment" (or recall) and the limitation on terms of office.

How often should leadership change in a human services organization? What is a reasonable time limit? Obviously, the protocol for administrative turnover should allow for reasonable time in an office to capture the benefits of the experience. Again, our political wisdom has suggested two successive terms in office or an eight-year period for the President of the United States is adequate. For the sake of operationalizing this principle, let's say eight years in an administrative post is sufficient to capture the value of experience without incurring the aforementioned disadvantages of life-tenure arrangements.

This principle certainly presents some new dilemmas as to how we reward administrative positions. People get used to status and money associated with higher positions. In fact, social workers with the same education and number of years' experience may differ as much as $10,000 a year in salary because one has an administrative position. An even greater difference in income can be expected between line workers and top agency administrators, between classroom teachers and superintendents of education. It is often this lure of increased financial security that tempts family therapists who love their work to abandon clients to become an administrator.

We also love the status an administrative position gives us. The worker who stays in the agency many years without becoming an administrator is suspect if s/he has the credentials for the position. The hierarchial model supports the assumption that higher is better. If you have the chance to move up, you will.

The solutions to these problems are made more complicated by our rigid mind-set toward the authority of the position. To successfully eliminate this world-view and set the framework in which we can have leaders who occupy positions because of the abilities and their own merit, we must free our thinking to accept another viewpoint. We must begin to see each position as having its own place in the agency, and we must see the people in these positions as being there because the role expectations and the person's talents fit. We need to instill in people an enthusiasm for doing a job well, and to see the job for its own worth, not in terms of how high it is on the organizational chart or how much authority it represents compared with other positions.

The huge discrepancies in salary will have to be eliminated. While it seems reasonable that a person with more responsibility should be paid more, it is doubtful that they need to be paid that much more. If we reduced the disparities in status and money within and among the levels of positions in the agency, turnover and rotation would be less troublesome to the individual. If we were told when we were hired that this is the protocol of the agency, we could also prepare ourselves better for these changes.

We also want to emphasize that for administrators, as well as for workers, jobs should be defined in terms of what needs to be done, but not according to how these tasks should be accomplished. This will enable an individual to apply his/her own talents in the best way to get the job done.[2] One can follow all the rules well but not accomplish the goals. In a welfare organization, this can

"He never was one for fancy titles."

be seen in the administrator who sees to it that every rule is enforced, but who fails to promote humane services to the people who need the agency services. By evaluating the end result, we can encourage people to use their own imagination. As Schumacher said:

> In his urgent attempt to obtain reliable knowledge about his essentially indeterminate future, the modern man of action may surround himself by ever-growing mountains of factual data to be digested by ever-more wonderful mechanical contrivances; I fear that the result is little more than a huge game of make-believe and an ever more marvelous vindication of Parkinson's Law. The best decisions will still be based on the judgements of mature non-electronic brains possessed by men who have looked steadily and calmly at a situation and seen it whole. 'Stop, look, and listen' is a better motto than 'Look it up in the forecasts'[3]

The professionalization of agency administration is one thing, but the institutionalization of the professional manager is quite another. The former can lead to improved agency direction. The latter, ultimately, frustrates it. This is another way of stating that we disagree with the attempt to functionally specialize "administrative leadership". As we have suggested, leadership needs to be "generalized" throughout the agency. We want all persons to be preparing for new leadership roles and for providing leadership in their current role. The best way to assure this is to create maximum opportunity for this to occur. Administrative turnover is one means of creating this opportunity.

Chapter VII

Notes

1. Dr. Laurence J. Peter and Raymond Hull, <u>The Peter Principle.</u>
<u>Why Things Always Go Wrong</u> (New York: Bantam Books, 1972).

2. Albert Cherns, "The Principles of Sociotechnical Design",
<u>Human Relations</u>, Volume 29, Number 8, 1976, p.786.

3. E.F. Schumacher, <u>Small is Beautiful. Economics as if People</u>
<u>Mattered</u> (New York: Harper Colophon Books, 1975), p.226.

CHAPTER VIII

PRINCIPLE OF PRIMARY COMMUNICATION

> Use (memoranda) for dissemination of noncontroversial
> information. Write them to yourself to organize your
> thoughts. But keep in mind that a memo is really a
> one-way street. There's no way to reply to it in
> real-time, or to engage it in a dialogue. Murder-by-
> memo is an acceptable crime in large organizations. . .
>
> Robert Townsend

One of the symbols of bureaucracy recognized by all is the memo. The familiar "To:, From:, Re:" is the common way for us to communicate with each other in bureaucratic organizations, but the piles of written messages that come over our desks become more loathesome than informative. In spite of the frustrations we feel with this written format, there must be a balance between the rational needs of traditional bureaucratic communication and the need of the human spirit to be talked with. To balance these needs in a theory of humanocracy, we must give substantial thought to the functions of communication in organizations and look for an alternative which relies less on the coldness of the interoffice memos.

Peter Drucker cites one function of communication in The Practice of Management: information must be fed to decision-makers before these managers can determine organizational policy. The Board of Directors cannot decide to lay off workers without having production and sales figures. Agency directors cannot budget funds for staff

without information about size of caseload. Large scale bureaucracies
are totally dependent for their survival on gathering, transmitting
and processing information. This flow of information is the life
blood of the organization. Communication is necessary for an organization to meet its goals.

Another function of communication is to provide the means by
which organizations as social systems can adapt to their environments.
The organization must adapt if it is to survive; agencies must respond
to community needs. Information must be brought into the system and
disseminated rationally and quickly. This involves not only
transmitting facts, but also interpreting the meaning of the information, responding as an organization, and giving out information. When
a protective services agency learns that one of the families it had
investigated had abused a child until s/he died, the agency must
quickly: 1) assimilate the information, 2) be sure that all members
of the agency who have had contact with the case have the same
information, 3) make a decision about the agency's public response to
the community it is accountable to, and 4) put out the information
that it feels best represents the agency's official position. To
make a response quickly enough to satisfy public demand, the agency
must already have an effective communication system in operation.

A communication system must link the interdependent parts of
the organizations. When a system is in dynamic balance, a change
in one part of the organization will produce an effect in all other
parts of that system. Therefore, the information in the communication network has the potential of affecting the total organization.

It is imperative that people throughout the agency have all the necessary information to be able to make specific, timely decisions at various levels of the hierarchy, and then be able to coordinate these decisions with other interrelated parts of the system. Information management, therefore, becomes an essential function of the organization and usually accounts for large expenditures of human and financial resources.

Communication is also the process by which the social development needs of the individual within the organization can be met. The agency newsletter, the numerous bulletins posted throughout the buildings, many of the general interest memoranda have all been witnesses to the fact that human beings must have information about their environment to function effectively. There are also items designed to build agency morale--announcement of the formation of a baseball team, the recognition of one unit's success with car pooling, the praise of a group of people in the organization who sponsored a fund raiser to help out a family. These communications convey the message that the organization offers the opportunity for a person to become involved with others in relationships other than those dictated by the job.

Not only is communication the means for meeting goals, it is itself a major goal. Once an organization has decided who will make what kinds of decisions, a major organizational goal becomes directing information flow in such a way that the decision makers have the necessary information. The communication system of an agency that relies on participatory decision-making will differ noticeably from one that has a policy of reducing the number of decision-makers to a few top administrators. If we are to propose a principle of humanocracy that offers an alternative to the regimentation of communication by written documents, we must include in our proposal a recognition that communication is always a crucial goal of any social system.

Humanocracy must also consider the patterns that communication networks have taken and what needs these patterns meet. One way of analyzing communication patterns is by the structure of information flow. These patterns are not an independent process, but rather are a reflection of the character of the organization. Once an organization defines its overall goals and objectives and organizes its structure, its communication system naturally flows from this definition of the organization. The communication system is a reflection of agency policy, not a separate activity that operates according to universal rules.

The traditional bureaucratic form of transmitting information is to move it through channels in the hierarchy. Within this communication network, information goes through a sequence by which messages are passed among people in the organization until they reach their final destination. Case and Boren have described changes in messages that go through this serial process:

(a) Details become omitted, declining sharply in number at the beginning of the series and continuing throughout thereafter, but at a somewhat slower rate (sometimes called leveling).

(b) Details, when retained, become highlighted, allowing them to gain in importance and meaningfulness (sometimes called sharpening).

(c) Details become added for the purpose of embellishing the description of the message.

(d) Details become modified to conform to the predisposition of the interpreter (sometimes called the simulation).

(e) Statements that were previously qualified tend to become definite statements and later reproductions.

(f) Details tend to become combined into a single, unitary concept. For example, what starts out as three individuals becomes, in a later reproduction, a "group" (sometimes called condensation).

(g) Details of the events or happenings are described in the order in which one would expect them to occur, rather than as they actually did occur.

(h) Details are adapted to make the entire message or event seem plausible.

(i) Finally, certain phrases are adjusted to reflect the accepted style of expression used by the social stratum of the individuals collectively involved in the reproduction of the message.[2]

To counteract these changes characteristic of serial communication, we have experimented with the direction of the flow of information. Students of bureaucracies categorize these directions into upward, downward, and horizontal networks of communication. The dominant form of communication flow is, again, determined by the philosophy

Piane   Look

of the organization. The most common form is that of downward

communication, information flowing from superiors and subordinates.

Most downward communication provides:

    a. directions for what is to be done

    b. goals that subordinates are to achieve

    c. discipline measures

    d. questions that subordinates are to answer, and

    e. policies that subordinates are to follow.

This downward communication will proceed along the established

lines of authority in the hierarchy, flowing neatly through the formal

patterns of network relationships.

One problem with downward communication is the process of

filtering. As was described earlier, the problem of the serial nature

of communication is that it either becomes changed, shortened,

lengthened, and/or distorted in some fashion as it flows through a

network. Filtering occurs because of the number of links in the

network, the perceptual differences among the employees, and a lack

of trust among persons. All of these variables may act as blocks

in relating or understanding messages; therefore, because of the

hierarchy, downward communication is a problem area for organizations.

Flow of communication down through an organization also begs the

problem of message overload. In many organizations, persons are over-

burdened with bulletins, memos, letters, announcements, magazines,

policy statements, and so forth. A highly selective screening process

must be instituted to protect employees from being overloaded, and

consequently filing important messages in the wastebasket.

Upward communication refers to information which flows from
subordinates to superiors, usually for the purposes of asking questions,
providing feedback and making suggestions. Upward communication
generally has the effect of improving morale and employee attitudes
and "serves as feedback for management. In addition...upward communication can stimulate employees to participate in formulating operating
policies for their department or organization". Management should
value upward communication because, as pointed out by Plant and
Machaver: (1) it indicates the receptivity of the environment to
downward communication; (2) it facilitates acceptance of decisions
by encouraging subordinate participation in the decision-making process;
(3) it provides feedback about subordinates' understanding the downward
communication; and (4) it encourages the submission of valuable ideas.[3]
Upward communication is valuable also as a means of satisfying basic
human needs (sense of personal worth, release of emotional tensions)
and is fundamental to a democratic method of decision-making. Methods
commonly used to implement upward communication include grievance
systems, rap sessions, open door policies, suggestion systems, opinion
surveys, employees' letters, and social gatherings.

Two major problems with upward flow include filtering and status.
Employees tend to send upward messages which enhance their credibility
and status, but they block or filter out those messages which may
make them look bad. Furthermore, Read has concluded, that the more
upward mobility aspirations an employee has, the less he will tell
his boss.[4] Besides the tendency to filter bad news as it travels
upward, the problem of status also inhibits many upward-directed
messages. Davis explained this problem:

A manager often does not realize how great the upward communication barrier can be, especially for blue collar work. His status and prestige at the plant are different from the workers. He probably talks differently and dresses differently. He can freely call a worker to his desk or walk to his work station, but the worker is not equally free to call in his manager. The worker usually lacks the ability to express himself as clearly as the manager. Who is better trained for practice in his communication skills... The worker is further impeded because he is not talking to a man with whose work and responsibilities he is familiar. The result is that very little upward communication occurs unless management positively encourages it.[5]

Horizontal communication is the lateral exchange of information among people on the same organizational level of authority. Research by Burns, Katz, Kahn, and DeWhirst among others have identified several purposes for communicating horizontally in an organization.[6] These include (1) information sharing, (2) problem-solving, (3) task coordination, and (4) conflict resolution. One model of horizontal communication was proposed in 1916 by Fayol[7]:

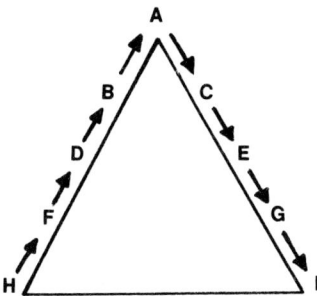

Communication flows according to a classical management approach. "F" talks to "G" by going through "A."

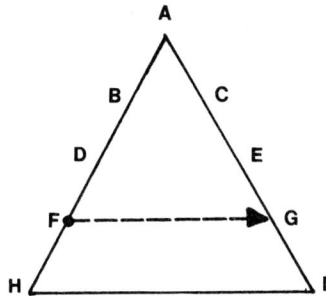

In Fayol's bridge for horizontal communication, "F" talks directly to "G".

The message now travels by way of one relay which will increase both accuracy and speed of travel. One wonders why there is not more widely applied unilateral communication throughout every organization. Several problems, however, have been stated in answer to this query.

1. One fear of bureaucratic managers is that if all people talk to all others whenever they wanted to, the authority structure would be abolished. There is need for some authority to effectively accomplish the system's goal and to coordinate the different specialty areas within the organization.

2. Another problem associated with the wide use of Fayol's "bridge" to all possible members of the organization, is message overload. Too many messages would flow in all direction without screening or filtering. As a result, the system might slow down and even cease to function from the burden of too much information.

3. There is concern about disruption from rivalry due to the competition among members of the organization. Some groups in the organization may either distort information or conceal it to meet their own self-interest.

4. In highly complex organizations with numerous divisions based on carrying out particular tasks, specialization results in the lack of a common language and value system with which people can communicate.

5. There is a lack of rewards and a resulting lack of motivation for people in bureaucratic organizations to communicate horizontally.

6. Horizontal communication is directly affected by organizational scale. As organizations increase in size and complexity, there are many more layers through which communication must travel. Consequently, there is more opportunity for distortion and/or lack of face-to-face contact among persons.

In spite of these problems, Fayol's model does offer a compromise between the rigidity of zero horizontal communication and the chaos of total horizontal message flow.

A final approach to the study of the roles of communication in bureaucratic organizations is to analyze the types of communication systems. Thayer identifies three such systems he believes are found in all organizations: (1) operational tasks or operations-related data; (2) regulatory (orders, rules, instructions) and (3) maintenance/ development (public and employee relations, advertising, training). Information flow within these three communication systems complete four necessary functions within organizations: to inform, to regulate, to persuade, and to integrate.[8]

Operational task messages relate to the desired goals of the organization, such as the services or specified activities which are of concern to the system. Task messages include giving organizational participants all the information necessary for them to efficiently complete their task. These would include activities such as training, orientation, problem-solving, brainstorming, and goal setting. Maintenance information relates to the achievement of the organizational outcome; whereas, task information relates to the content of the system output. Maintenance information helps the organization to remain viable and to perpetuate itself (such as policy or regulation).

Regulatory messages include commands, dictates, procedures, orders and controls necessary to facilitate the organization's movements toward its goal. This is directed at people within the organizations - their attitudes, satisfactions, and fulfillment, and is concerned with feelings, inter-personal relationships, self-concept and individual morals. It would include praise of organizational participants, grapevine activities as well as conflict resolution, information and counseling sessions. Such information is crucial to the overall morale of the organization.

It is our belief that the very design of the bureaucracy makes communication among persons difficult. This design, which managers believe must be accompanied by classical organizational management practices, presents key barriers in developing meaningful interpersonal communication networks which can further the social development needs of persons within the organization. The rational managers of bureaucratic organizations focus on organizational communication as it involves messages, their flow, the purpose, the directions, and the media. There is a heavy reliance on written and "hard" methods of communications, such as expensive manuals, newspapers, and public address systems.

Bureaucratic managers somehow seem to ignore the reality that organizational communication also involves people, their attitudes, feelings, relationship, and skills. While too much or too little communication may be a problem humorously portrayed in cartoons and fictionalized essays, an equally important and more often overlooked problem is the manager's propensity to ignore the fact that communication is a very personal and individual experience. Communication behavior will be different between two people when confronted by a common stimuli since past experience as well as physiology influence one's perception. Is it any wonder that workers, coming into the organization with a background of experiences unique to each person, become bureau-neurotic when constantly being talked to as if all members of the group were alike?

The division of labor also compounds communication problems. Everyone knows that the people at the point of the triangular chart talk with outsiders, especially those representing the press or the group to which the organization is most accountable. By adhering strictly to this rule, we compound the anxiety described in the preceding chapters by implanting in workers' minds that outsiders are suspect, and only those "in the know" can mediate the boundaries. In reality, all members of the organization are linked with other systems and thus represent the agency. The use of communication as an axe of power is so contrary to reality that the individual finds it difficult to adjust to the dissonance the situation creates.

An atmosphere for bureau neurosis is encouraged by the limited communication from worker to manager. We know from research that information is distorted as it flows through the organizational structure. Consequently, the higher in a hierarchy, the more decisions must be based on less and less detail. This occurs because messages

lose detail as they are relayed through organizational networks--a
process called "uncertainty absorption" by March and Simon.[9] Great
emphasis on the design and development of complex management information
systems tries to counteract this tendency with complex information
retrieval system, but the reality of personal experience cannot
be so easily punched onto computer tape. While such sophisticated
technology can be of tremendous use, the repeated summaries necessitated
by putting decision-making higher and higher along the hierarchy
still distort reality. Often these decisions made by managers with
elaborate cost-benefits analyses are absurd to the persons who must
implement them. The worker is assured by a written document that
this was a rationally made decision, at the same time the worker
can see that the plan won't work. Continued emphasis on this upward
flow of information through several levels of managers, and the
resulting downward flow of memoranda dictating action, will insure
poor decisions.

Another example of a rational approach to communication that
goes astray when adhered to by strict classical managers is the focus
on formal communication matched with a determination to ignore the
powerful grapevine. We know that informal messages exist. They
develop through the informal associations of people, special matching
of personalities, and close proximity of people to each other. The
term "grapevine" applies to all informal communication. (The term
originated in the days of the Civil War, when Intelligence telegraph
lines were strung loosely from tree to tree in a manner of a grapevine.
The message thereon was often garbled; hence, any rummor was said

to be from the grapevine.) Research on the grapevine conducted by Jacobsen and Seashore, Walter, Sutton and Porter has produced the following finds [10]:

(a) The grapevine is personal. Since the grapevine does not follow formal channels, it is usually more personal in its transmission, and the messages are free to travel as fast as the sender and receivers desire. Davis reports that in one organization, 46% of the management group knew about one manager's new born child within thirteen hours after the event. Walton also reports the grapevine to be the speediest channel for spreading messages among employees.

(b) The Grapevine is active. By counting the details of messages and determing which are true and false, Davis was able to report an accuracy ranging from 80-90% for non-controversial company information. [11] In a study of the U.S. Naval Ordinance Test Station, Walton found that about 78% of the employees tested thought the information on the grapevine was correct at least half of the time; however, they generally believed that grapevine information transmission is inaccurate because of some inaccuracy of information. Situations which tend to be anxious or exciting may affect the accuracy of the grapevine, but overall its track record is quite good.

(c) The grapevine carries a great deal of information. Grapevine transmission of the information of an organization is a fact of life within all organizations. The grapevine offers a network for defusing some messages which cannot normally be sent over formal networks. The grapevine also provides feedback to management about employees sentiment, and provides an outlet for expressing emotionally-charged messages which, if not expressed, may foster growing hostility and anger among employees. Lastly, the grapevine may help translate some of the management's directives into language easily understood by employees.

The most negative attribute about grapevine communication is that it serves as a network over which rumors travel. Allport and Postman stated in their basic 'law of rumor' that the spreading of rumors is a function of both the importance and the ambiguity of the information pertaining to the topic at issue.[12] Workers who must rely on the grapevine for most information or for information they feel is most likely to directly affect their jobs, are more likely to suffer from bureau neurosis. If managers ignore the power of the grapevine and think that the only information that matters is the official, documented information, they can create an atmosphere where frustrated workers will look down on the naivete of their "superiors". Managers can admit to the power of the grapevine, and thus combat bureau neurosis with an open attitude toward sharing information whenever possible.

The problems of communication in large organization can be destructive to both the goals of the system and to the human needs of the people in the organization. The proposal we put forth to alleviate some of the problem created by the over emphasis on rationality and formality is the Principle of Primary Communication.

Primary communication means talking with others whenever possible
and necessary. While formal lines of relaying information may be
continued, people should also be encouraged to talk with others
informally, regardless of the placement of their roles in the organizational structure. We agree that one's role in an organization defines
to a considerable extent who one talks to about what ; however, a
person also communicates with others about both job-related and non-job
activities. This difference between formal and informal communication
channels within a network accounts for the communication which does
not follow the organizational chart.

The realities of informal communication should be a crucial
factor in information dissemination, not an interesting aside for
social scientists to study. If a member of the board recognizes
a workers, s/he should feel free to stop and talk about substantive
matters. If a major policy decision is being made, those making
the decision should not be afraid to sit down and discuss it with
line workers on coffee break. If friendships exist, they should
not be hidden. In other words, the organization can take into account
the reality that people will be human and will establish ties based
on their emotions. These emotional links should be as valid as the
lines on the organizational chart.

If people in the organization are going to talk to each other,
they should also listen. The all-knowing nod from a supervisor hearing
a line worker relate experiences with a new AFDC form can insult
the worker. Communication will cease, and the worker will simply
proceed to find ways of avoiding the problems by stepping around

agency rules. Maybe the supervisor doesn't listen, but the worker did and s/he read the message.

Supervisors aren't the only ones who are reluctant to listen to another perspective. Workers often enter a supervisor's office with an "I would like to discuss something with you" that is spoken to conceal the real agenda--to complain about a situation s/he doesn't understand. The supervisor's explanations and attempts to problem solve with the worker are consistently met with hostile "Yes, buts". The worker does not want to communicate, to understand, or to share perspectives. He only wants pity and retribution.

The Principle of Primary Communication is based on one of the basis premises of this book: organizations must not outgrow human scale. A study of any complex organization reveals dyadic and small group interactions which account for practically all of the human interaction in organizations. Within human service organizations, for example, most departments are composed of small groups. Meetings and many informal activites take place in dyads and small groups. Giving and receiving directions, information, rules, regulations, and plans, and even the spread of rumors, involve the interaction of only a few people. The aggregate of these combine to form a communication network, the pathways for the flow of information between and among people in the organization. If decision-making groups are kept small enough so that people can communicate informally, the formal communications will also be more valid.

The Principle of Primary Communication is not a plea to abandon the written word. The memoranda, the newsletter, and the contract

O prudent bureaucracy! Thy cannons shall have their bowels
full of paper. And ready mounted are they to split forth
their rain of memos that thou shalt stand as sovereign and
vanquisher.

James H. Boren - <u>When</u> <u>in</u> <u>Doubt,</u> <u>Mumble</u>

have a place in a rational, ordered world. There must be a balance between the use of written and spoken words. The prudent manager must carefully select information, and then print only the relevant materials that are best communicated in writing. This represents a key decision-making problem for all persons with the organization.

A social service organization must not only strive for efficiency but must address the social development needs of its human resources in order to remain viable. Efforts to increase direct communication among persons should be made in order to more adequately meet the social needs of people and thus reduce unnecessary rational and impersonal climates. We continue to argue that when the emotional needs of people are taken into account, the rational goals of the organization will be better met.

Chapter VIII

Notes

1. Peter Drucker, Practice of Management (New York: Harper & Row, 1954), p. 346.

2. R.W. Case and R. Boren, The Human Transaction (Glenview, IL: Scott Foresman Co., 1973).

3. Earl Plant and William Machaver, "Upward Communications: A Project in Executive Development", Personnel, 28-4 (1952), 304-18.

4. William H. Read, "Upward Communication in Industrial Hierarchies", Human Relations 15-1 (1962): 3-15.

5. Keith Davis, "Management Communication and the Grapevine", Harvard Business Review 31 (September-October, 1953): 43-49.

6. Tom Burns, "The Directions of Activity and Communication in a Department Executive Group", Human Relations 7 (1954): 73-97; Daniel Katz and Robert Kahn, The Social Psychology of Organizations (New York: John Wiley & Sons, Inc., 1966); and H.D. DeWhirst, "Influence of Perceived Information Sharing Norms on Communication Channel Utilization", Academy of Management Journal 14 (1971), 305-15.

7. Henri Fayol, General and Industrial Management, Trans. Constance Starrs (London: Pitman, 1949).

8. Lee Thayer, Communications and Communication Systems (Homewood, IL: Richard D. Irwin, 1968).

9. James March and Hervert Simon, Organizations (New York: John Wiley and Sons, Inc., 1966).

10. Eugene Jacobsen and Stanley Seashore, "Communication Practices in Complex Organizations", Journal of Social Issues, 7(1951): 28-40; Eugene Walton, "How Efficient is the Grapevine?" Personnel 28 (1961): 45-49; H. Sutton and L. Porter, "A Study of the Grapevine in a Governmental Organization", Personnel Psychology 21-22 (1968) 223-30.

11. Keith Davis, "A Human Behavior at Work", Personnel Psychology 6(1953): 301-12.

12. Gordon Allport and Leo Postman, The Psychology of Rumor (New York: Henry Holt & Co., 1947).

CHAPTER IX

THE PRINCIPLE OF DESIGN PSYCHOLOGY

> There are two sorts of habitation in Africa. One is of
> brick, cement, plaster, tile and tin--the substance of
> the country processed and shaped; the other sort is made
> direct of the stuff of soil and grass and tree. . . . A
> house like this is a living thing, responsive to every
> mood of the weather; and during the time I was growing
> up it had already begun to sink back into the forms of
> the bush. I remember it as a rather old, shaggy animal
> standing still among the trees, lifting its head to look
> out over the hills and valleys to the mountains....The
> fact is, I don't live anywhere; I never have since I
> left that first house on the Kopje.

Doris Lessing

Doris Lessing computed that she had lived in over sixty different

dwellings, but she had been at home in only one - "the old, shaggy

animal" that her family had built with their own hands from the

materials around them. The frame was of the trees, held together

by a wet and slippery substance from other trees. This was covered

with mud from an ant-heap. The roof was made from the best and tallest

grass on the farm. The floor was more mud, covered with fresh cow/dung

and wetted with clear water and fresh blood of an ox. The house

smelled sweet earth smells and formed a union with the family and

the land.[1] Such is the ultimate of design psychology - the shaping

of an environment to meet the needs and reflect the personalities

of the people who will inhabit the space.

The shaping of space is one of the tools management has that

can most dramatically humanize an organization. The physical environment is at once a reflection of the organization's values, its priorities and its administrative philosophy. It speaks as clearly about the organization as clothes do about the person who wears them. And like clothes, the physical dimension can add to or detract from the comfort levels of those who must function within its space.

What do our human service offices say about us and our attitudes toward the services we deliver and the people who receive them? The physical environments of many human service organization workplaces can be likened to a stage for a theatre of the absurd. The nation's center for determining mental health policy conducts its work in tiny cubicles, in a stainless steel and glass megastructure, surrounded by acres of concrete parking. People in this building serve as the gate keeper of our nation's collective mental health. This phenomenon is not unique. Those concerned with the care of the elderly at the federal level spend their work days in spaces more aged and disregarded than the elderly whom they struggle to serve. From the dingy basement of a courthouse, many county social workers must first overcome the barriers of their location before they can care for the poor.

It is as if we had consciously engineered absurdity into many of our service environments. Modern junior high schools look more like giant water closets than contemporary learning centers. Many have been designed without windows, lest they be broken. Major urban hospitals resemble huge computers with beds. With so much medical hardware, there remains little space left for patients, let alone

their families. Whatever happened to the hospital arrangement where
families slept in and comforted their sick relative? Even modern
marketing places suggest that more care is given to parking automobiles
than to comforting human bodies. And so it goes in the world's
wealthiest of nations.

We owe much credit to Frederick Taylor for our assembly-line
mentality toward environmental design.[2] For him, an organization
had but one purpose: efficient production. People, like machines,
were largely instruments in the production process. Worker comfort
and safety were not highly regarded in his view of the organization
of the work place. Though Taylor's concepts are a half-century old,
a study of the environments of many social agencies would appear
to be predicated on his principles. How else can we explain the dis-
regard of worker and client comfort and well being in many of our
modern social welfare institutions?

The human service agency, as it embraces the philosophies and
views of modern organizational theory, has increasingly leaned toward
an assembly-line approach to service delivery. The plastic environments
of the fast food establishments are fast becoming the equally plastic
environment of other service organizations. Economy is but one factor
that explains this trend. At a deeper level, the management perspective
has become one of how to interface man with a machine to increase
productivity; however, few administrators realize the extent to which
they have subjugated their employees to machine technology.

There is a marvelous office scene in an old movie. The
Millionaire in which a multimillionaire gives away his
fortune to people he has picked at random from the phone
directory. A clerk, played by Charles Laughton, sits at
a desk in an enormous, drab room filled with row upon row
of identical desks. A letter arrives. He opens it and
finds a check for a million dollars. He looks at it briefly,
rises, and lumbers up the aisle past his co-workers, all
of whom have their noses buried in their work. The camera
follows him as he opens one door after another, each of
which has a bigger nameplate than the previous one, until
he finally arrives at the door marked "President." He bangs
it open, sticks his head in, puts out his tongue, and
makes a huge, fat, noisy raspberry.

Albert Mehrabian - Public Places and Private Spaces

The assembly line has traditionally served as a metaphor for the dehumanization of the human factor in its interface with machines. From Charlie Chaplin's "City Lights" to Kurt Vonnegut's "Piano Player"[3], the story has been told over and over again. The tragedy is that the assembly line is not only found in the bowels of Detroits and Akrons these days. Its counterpart, the social assembly line, is to be found in most large public and private service agencies throughout the post-industrial world. Frederick Weisman's visual presentation of New York City's welfare organization is little different from Chaplin's "City Lights", in spite of the differences in time and location. In fact, Weisman's similar drama documentaries of "High School","Tilticult Follies", and "Hospitals"[4], were a replay of the same theme - dehumanization in the service agencies.

The interiors of our service megastructures look decidedly the same. Organizational furnishings -- albeit in hospitals, schools or social agencies -- seem to have been selected from a single supplier with a one-product line. Like Holiday Inns, our human service organizations appear to take pride in the predictability and standardization of their furnishings. The concept of interior design has become "institutionalized", almost stereotyped. The fact that this has happened is an indication of either benign neglect or lack of a management vision toward the workplace. In either case, it is a failure to understand and appreciate how a work environment can affect worker morale and productivity.

Acceptance of such cold, plastic environments is not necessary. We can create warmer space that reflects our spirit and our philosophy.

Within the constraints of the dollar and, ocassionally, public opinion, we can do almost anything we want with our work spaces, if management will permit it. Management must first recognize the power of a well-designed environment in maximizing both productivity and worker-client well being. Next it must develop a theory of design psychology to guide its actions. It is not as if management persons lacked an appreciation of design, since many have taken great care to provide themselves with comfortable and workable quarters. Management need only extend to their workers and clients what they have provided for themselves.

A plea of scarce resources won't do. Money alone is not the issue. The same amount of money can be used to shape space creatively as to institutionalize it. Certainly, Doris Lessing's home of sticks, grass and mud was not an expensive house. It cost no money, but it was valuable to the family because it was created by them. We can also shape our spaces for little money.

Architects speak of this physical dimension of our organizations as the "designed environment" or the "man-built" environment. Whatever the nature of the space in which we work or seek services, such environments don't just happen. The people who use the space put it together and continue to modify it. Our concern is the underlying "theory" that explains how and why it is put together as it is. Who designed it, and for what purpose? Again, this should make us think about the fundamental purposes of our service organizations. Is a school to be exclusively designed as a learning environment? Is a prison to be designed solely for the deterrence of its criminal inhabitants?

Is the social agency to be designed totally for the efficient production
of a social service?

If we take efficient production of a service as the sole purpose
of a social agency, then the Frederick Taylor's time-motion study
might make more sense. But, if there is more to organizational life,
such as the comfort and well-being of its participants, then there
needs to be more to the design of its physical arrangements. Under
a theory of humanocracy there must be greater balance in the design
and organization of the environment between efficient productivity
and human development.

Let's explore more deeply the concept of design psychology.
What must be done to create a comfortable and workable environment?
An answer lies in what most people have done with their home environments. As an architectural friend of ours points out, humans, like
other animals, have strong nesting instincts. Given the opportunity
(and in some instances, a little encouragement) individuals will
build tasteful, comfortable, even productive "nests". In a five-year
experiment in the School of Social Work at The University of Iowa,
faculty were free to do what they wanted to their areas, while being
encouraged by administration to express themselves and share themselves
through their design choices. The results were delightful. No two
offices were alike. Most were filled with favorite furnishings from
the occupant's home. Personal items, such as pictures, posters,
sculpture, plants, etc. were added in every case. In several instances,
the traditional office desk was foregone for a more workable table,
often an old, but refinished dining table. The faculty went even

farther by sharing special items for the general areas of the School as well. Through the creation of a small foundation, the faculty invested in some antique furnishings that served as the school's center pieces. All of these items continue to grow in value, while servicing the School's needs. One item, a large roll-top desk, purchased for $200 five years ago, has appreciated $500 in value in this time.

Implementing the principle of design psychology is little more than respecting this nesting instinct of workers and clients and producing arrangements that contribute to human development. In other words, management needs to respond to the basic needs of people who share in its space, if any sort of real productivity is to occur. We are aware, of course, of the universality of our basic needs for identity, individualization, positive self-concept, affection, security and challenge. Thoughtful design arrangements can make positive moves to meeting these needs, with equally positive outcomes in the releasing of energy for work. Feelings of physical discomfort have rarely heightened work output; they have contributed to bureau neurosis.

In mental hospitals, for example, it has been the practice to take personal possessions from a patient at admission and to immediately respond to the patient in his new identity as that of a mentally ill person. This is efficient in the sense that it makes patient compliance and management easier. Yet, it assaults the person's already fragile ego. It "institutionalizes" the person when the opposite is really what is needed in mental health treatment.

The mental health work force is rarely better off than their patients. Encased in stereotyped uniforms, closeted behind impersonal nursing stations, working in crowded corridors and wards, the psychiatric work group goes about its various tasks, which in and of themselves are often enervating. The work is made even more difficult because of the alienating features of the environment. The cafeterias of even most modern hospitals are noisy, plastic environments, serving prepared foods that are modeled after the fast food establishments. Foods prepared hours earlier rest dutifully under the artificial heat of a fluorescent light waiting to be hurriedly eaten by workers whose lunchtime escapes hold little reward. Men and women in white coats, with their face masks still dangling from their necks, gobble down second-rate food before returning to their life-sustaining tasks in the surgery room.

In schools, students and their teachers hurriedly gulp down their food, so the next group of students and faculty can occupy their table and chairs 30 minutes later. Seventh graders are herded to the lunch room by 11:15 a.m. so that the ninth graders can be served by 12:30 p.m. whether they are hungry at that hour or not. Little wonder we feel so much harrassment in our workdays in the service agencies. Blue-collar workers have won through union negotiations mid-day work breaks -- human service workers have not.

The social assembly-line needs to be replaced with a work pattern and work flow that integrates individual needs with work requirements and organizational needs. The social agency is the home away from home for both the workers and their clients. For clients in long-term care situations - mental hospitals, nursing homes, chronic hospitals, residential treatment centers - our workplace is, in fact, their "home". Their home should not be our social assembly line. Our work efficiency is not justification for usurping the design to favor organizational needs over personal living needs.

Our point, as we have repeatedly stated, is the need for balance between design efficiency and design psychology in the overall design of the agency. The resources we have to work with must be distributed fairly in building such a balanced environment. A service environment need not be an architectural monument, but only a simple, comfortable, personal, human setting where the quality and concern of the service enterprise is fully manifested through appropriate physical design arrangements.

Until the variable of the physical design of the workplace is elevated to a level of a management principle, it will continue to be neglected. While we can offer no magic formula or even much data for producing positive psychological effects, we can suggest that administrators become aware of the importance of environmental design. In the absence of any more definitive suggestions, we would argue for giving the worker ample freedom to construct a nesting place, reflecting his or her personal identity and individuality, and involving some personal artifacts from the worker's own treasure of personal possessions.

Recently we assisted a rural county welfare agency in moving out of the courthouse basement into a simple, prefabricated metal building. The county board of supervisors had placed a dollar limit on what could be constructed, which necessitated the choice of the prefabricated building. Yet, the workers had been instructed in the concept of design psychology and were given administrative licence to do what they pleased with the interior design and organization. Left alone, the workers brought plants, wall hangings, radios, coffee pots, pictures, posters, toys, novelties, and the like. The result was a warm, engaging environment where workers felt relaxed and clients felt wanted. The cost: human energy and creativity. The dollars needed were negligible.

While the principle of design psychology is largely undiscovered, we hope that future humanists will redress this gap. Such a simple license as freeing people to design their immediate surroundings can do much to relieve bureau neurosis.

Chapter IX

Notes

1. Doris Lessing, Going Home (New York: Popular Library, 1957) pp. 29-34.

2. Frederick Taylor, Scientific Management (New York: Harper and Row, 1947).

3. Charlie Chaplin, City Lights, 1931.

4. Kurt Vonnegut, Piano Player (New York: Dela Court Press), 1952.

5. Frederick Weisman, Tilticult Follies, 1967; Hospitals, 1969; High School, 1968.

CHAPTER X

PRINCIPLE OF SUBJECTIVITY

Ninety-two is a silly age
I'm a foolish old man, laughing
To keep from dying.

Busy Work!
I won't do that dizzy work
I didn't live through 70 hard years
To make potholders.

I'm an individual
Don't call me "we".

"We" don't want to go to the bathroom
"We" don't want to eat my nice dinner
"We" won't take my medicine
Even if it is good for "us".

"We've" got you fooled, Nurse.
You think I'm contrary
I would do what you want, Miss
If you would only ask me.

Julia Houy, "Ramblings."

Human service workers have held to a value system that places emphasis on the individual "I", but we have organized our services into agencies that serve the conglomerate "we". Service providers hide behind this editorial "we" to prove a hollow professionalism characterized by objectivity toward the very people we value as unique individuals. Is it any wonder that we develop bureau neurosis trying to function with such dissonance built into our organizations? It is not only "foolish old men" in nursing homes[1] whom we try to objectify; we impose this principle of objectivity on all clients and on our co-workers.

A humanistic approach to administration is not compatible with this principle of objectivity; but when adding an alternative principle as part of a theory of humanocracy, we run some major risks. What will be said here definitely flies in the face of conventional organizational wisdom and practice. Part of the religion of bureaucracy has been a belief in objectivity and impersonal decision-making. To the large organizational theorist objectivity is the conduct of organizational life in a disciplined, unprejudicial, impersonal manner, where individual idiosyncracy is largely overlooked in favor of common generic attitudes towards any individuals involved in the organizations' functioning. Demography is acknowledged; human personality is not.

The basis for the origin of this principle is apparent, particularly in government organization. At about the mature point of the Industrial Revolution, when organizations were growing larger and showing monopolistic tendencies and local governments were found guilty of corruption and boss control, theorists argued for an organizational design that would reduce, if not eliminate, "favoritism" and "being bought". It fit nicely into the educational design and practice of the growing professional class, which given the opportunity of more "limited" human involvement with their clients and/or patients, seem to choose it. Even social workers were admonished by their teachers and supervisors "not to get too close to their clients" nor show more than "controlled" emotional involvement. So, we converted an organizational approach into a virtuous act. Our legacy is that today we deny applications for Food Stamps, reject students from

"It's for you."

The Washington Post
April 22, 1981

admission to graduate school, keep aliens out of the country, and conduct life threatening operations with sanctimonious objectivity.

Objectivity has a peculiar dynamic; however, one cannot function from a position of controlled emotional involvement or general bureaucratic impersonalness without doing something rather powerful to the client. Detachment, however mild, means one necessarily misses the nuances of the client life that are critical to any assessment process. When we are objective, we de-personalize the client; and, when we de-personalize the client, we are in effect treating him/her as a thing - an object. It is as if to say that to be objective is to relate to another as if s/he were an object.

It was this apparent drift of de-personalization in the early 20th century in industrial Europe and America that gave rise to the existentialist movement and the inward search for meaning and the self-recognition of one's personhood and uniqueness. It is as if when social institutions quit helping persons experience their individual identity, the individual fell back into a self protective, self-limiting way of life.

Tragically, the tools created for use in the post-industrial world accelerated our dependency upon objective approaches to organizational life. The computer's limitations are such that it cannot deal with the individual aspects of human psychology, as it deals so easily with the aggregate's human demographics. Our institutions, therefore, have become services geared to populations, not to persons. Since we are dealing with a problem shared by many, our solution will be a solution geared to many. To assure productivity and efficiency, we must reduce the complexity of the problem by treating our client group in some kind of summary way--finding the common denominator. Not unexpectedly the common denominator is often the point at which a society is willing to spend money to address the problem. Typically, funding is far below what is actually needed.

Where has objectivity brought us? To be objective one must invent and put into place some sort of barrier between workers and clients. The basic lack of trust in humans in bureaucracies could never allow us to depend on discretion, judgement, intuition, love, and involvement in providing a service. So we substitute application forms, eligibility criteria, performance evaluations, time study reports, manuals of regulations, monthly reports, and audits. Layers and layers of paper help to de-personalize the client by turning his flesh into a set of statistics.

In the service area, there exists a kind of myth that getting involved with your client will rapidly burn you out; however, there is little research to support this. Worker burn-out is a condition which develops when workers no longer find themselves truly needed or engaged in meaningful activity. It occurs when we feel poorly understood and not regarded or recognized for our personal characteristics and our professional investments. It is not our relationship with our clients that burns us out. It is more likely to be the volumes of paper work designed to keep us objective.

Burn-out is also one of the consequences of bureau neurotic feelings. We think that to deal rationally with people, we must

... all of the animals in the world are psychologically less
distinct from one another than one man is from other men.

Gordon Allport - <u>Becoming</u>

be objective. But, we know intuitively as humans that we actually

deal with people subjectively. The conflict between the organization's

demand that we be rational and our own human emotions telling us

to "feel" for people we are trying to serve causes bureau neurosis.

The elaborate steps we take to remain objective only compound our

anxieties. It is not the emotional involvement with clients that

leads to burn-out; it is the very steps we take to remain objective

that contribute to our neurosis.

The alternative to objectivity that we propose is the Principle

of Subjectivity. This principle suggests that we function with respect

to others as if they were "subjects". This means to recognize and

respect that, while individuals share some common characteristics

with other individuals, their most distinctive feature is their

uniqueness.

It is human uniqueness and idiosyncracy that separates humans

from other living organisms. Gordon Allport once tried to develop

a theory of human psychology based on this singular trait of individual

idiosyncracy.[2] Allport presented as one of the fundamental needs

of human beings the need to be understood and treated with respect

for individual differences. As a matter of principle, our institutions

should be expected to develop rules, regulations, procedures and

protocols that acknowledge this reality.

Our model for subjectivity is the family, for only in the family

(occasionally in school) do we find ways of operating that take into

account the fact that no two people are alike. What is good for one person is not necessarily good for another. In schools, special "classes" are needed for learners who present different levels of intellectual and emotional readiness. In the home, individual negotiations are made daily to help foster the development of individual personality. Admittedly, even in the last remaining communal institution, the family, this is not always the case. There are certainly families which are run with the same bureaucratic rigidity as large organizations. The real question is whether large organizations can function like families. Can relationships be established among workers (and managers) that are designed to be mutually supportive, independent of how they articulate as part of the production line? Can procedures, protocols, etc., be developed that allow for individual differences and latitude for personal idiosyncracy? Can individual growth be viewed as much a product of the corporation as the other assembly line products? We think these humanizing ideals can be actualized.

As we cite in another chapter, bureaucratic organizations now design and furnish offices as if all persons had the same taste. The only differences are that we provide bigger space and more luxurious furnishings to the bosses, and we ocassionally allow those at the top to have some say over the decorations of the personal office. The principle of subjectivity would suggest that what's good for the "boss" is perhaps even better or more needed by organizational employees at the bottom of the status level. Subjectivity means allowing the human personality to flow freely in the organizational

environment, limited only by serious obtrusion into the personality
set of others who share the same organizational world and by the
parameters of the organization's goals.

A subjective approach to organizational management involves
many steps. The scale of the organization must be small enough
that people can get to know each other, workloads reasonable enough
that there is time to spend with one another, policies and procedures
which do not mandate treating everyone the same and an administrative
philosophy that assures that the spirit of this principle is truly
implemented.

The incumbent dangers associated with this principle are fairly
transparent. Can we become "more intimate" and still be fair and
equitable in our treatment of one another? Wouldn't we, in fact,
be more fair if we relied on our own intuitions rather than on the records
we know have been "doctored" to help the record keeper? We think
so. When responding to individuals, we may make some poor decisions;
but we have strong evidence that we are being less fair to people
operating under a principle of objectivity. Maybe more people would
do what needs to be done, "If you would only ask me." [3]

Chapter X

Notes

1. Julia Houy, "Ramblings", from Liguorian, reprinted in Elizabeth Ferguson, Social Work (Philadelphia: J.B. Lippincott Company, 1975), pp. 271-72.

2. Gordon Allport, Becoming (New Haven: Yale University Press, 1955).

3. Houy.

CHAPTER XI

PRINCIPLE OF CONVIVIALITY

> Tools are intrinsic to social relationships. An
> individual relates himself in action to his society
> through the use of tools that he actively masters, or
> by which he is passively acted upon. To the degree that
> he masters his tools, he can invest the world with his
> meaning; to the degree that he is mastered by his tools,
> the shape of the tool determines his own self-image.
> Convivial tools are those which give each person who
> uses them the greatest opportunity to enrich the
> environment with the fruits of his or her vision.

Ivan Illich

Tools should simplify our lives.[1] The most obvious ones are

machines -- cranes, cars, air hammers, microwave ovens -- but we

also have intangible tools that produce decisions, knowledge, and

services. Human services rely most heavily on these latter tools,

but we have made them so complicated to use that they are hardly

"tools".

One tool so characteristic of our agencies is the statement

of policy and procedures. Conceived to protect clients from the

wrath of unsympathetic workers by guaranteeing uniform rights,

these procedures have evolved into cumbersome red tape. Red tape has

become so common that it is now a standard word in the English language.

The concept has even warranted a study by the Brookings Institute's

Herbert Kaufman. Kaufman in 1977 wrote a short book titled Red Tape:

Its Origins, Uses and Abuses, in which he described the origins of

the term:

> Lexicographers seem to agree that the term red tape derives
> from the ribbon once used to tie up legal documents in
> England. Because the common law gives great weight to
> precedent, every judicial decision must have been preceded
> by a thorough search of the records for guidance and
> authority. Such a system presumes that records of every
> transaction are punctiliously filed and cross-filed. We
> may surmise, therefore, that legions of clerks and lawyers
> spent a good deal of their time tying and untying the
> ribbon-bound folders.[2]

Perhaps another word from the English language adds a certain

poetic flair to the concept - obfuscation. To obfuscate is to take

the simple or the intelligible and somehow make it complex and un-

intelligible. But why? To what purpose is organizational life served

by complex organizational arrangements, rules, regulations, procedures

and practices? Is there an organizational architect at work in the

bureaucracies' back room designing a maze built of paper to confuse

the wary consumer and, oftentimes the bureaucrats as well? The

answer cannot be that tying an agency and its clients into knots

of red tape is rational. Nor does it meet the emotional needs of

anyone involved. It is, in fact, one of the major causes of bureau

neurosis.

Perhaps one explanation is that our organizations, like Topsy,

"just growed".[3] As we continue to argue throughout this book, many

of the problems associated with bureaucracy, including organizational

complexity, are a function of scale and perhaps greediness towards

productivity and efficiency as organizational goals. The design

of complex electronic circuitry may make a computer do its thing

with efficiency and predictability; but when you transpose a human

circuitry of similar scale, it literally produces an electro-human

The smaller the size the less reason to have a Book to
go by, and the more chance for decency and common sense
to prevail. There is more chance of correcting a bad
practice when people, not the System, are responsible.

Harry Tripper, Jr. - The System and What You
Can Do With It

"blow-out" the sudden and complete collapse of real worker output.

We have added miles of red tape with each increase in agency size,

and now our workers and clients are hopelessly entangled in unnecessary

red tape.

Another tool of human services is the organization itself.

It is the people, organized in some rational arrangement of skills

and knowledge, that provides services. As Virginia Robinson urged,

it is the agency that can be orchestrated to help the client realize

his/her potential.[4] It is the totality of the school that can give

the child opportunities to learn. This unit, this system of skills

and knowledge, is a primary tool of human services.

But what have we done with this tool? It seems rather apparent

that by virtue of increasing the size and scale of organizations

that we have created the necessity for complicated organization.

This is particularly true when we take a highly rationalistic and

mechanistic view toward management and control. We create a chain

of command and a span of control that touches from top to bottom;

but, like so many "circuits", the flow of communication must be nearly

perfect from one point to another to assure valid communiques. A

little loss of information at each point can be disastrous, a major

disruption at any one point can be disabling; the confusion causes

bureau neurosis. The larger the organization, the more inevitable

is the probability that communication losses will occur. It is not

by coincidence that all major organizations rate "communication

problems" among their foremost problems. This is an artifact of

size and the numbers of human actors that are required to carry out the work of the organization.

We have also destroyed the usefulness of the organization as a tool, and compounded the problem of bureau neurosis by weighting workers down with agency policies, procedures, rules. The awareness of the reality that not all the folks in the organization are playing their part as prescribed (or at least management's suspicion that some are not) leads to an attempt to control for such deviance. The large organization must necessarily install a monitoring system. This can take many forms, varying from product control to personnel performance monitoring and evaluation. Succumbing to its predictable paranoia, the organization creates a system of inspection and compliance. Inevitably, this system requires a diversity of "paper controls". Based on a lack of trust, often well founded in a large organization, this system of accountability ranges from annoying to demoralizing the worker. And it adds tremendously to the complexity of organizational function and, of course, to organizational inefficiency (it takes a lot of time to fill out a lot of forms) and to worker/client confusion and demoralization.

The intentions behind a rational system of control, of making life in the organization both intelligible and governable, is honorable. Likewise, the responsible exercise of some measure of product and worker control and accountability is to be applauded. Rarely, however, does the large organization appear to be able to stop there. In the public bureaucracies every worker error or client advantage seems

to precipitate additional paper control. By legislating, we hope
to improve on the performance of the system, but with each new regulation and procedure we add to the organization's complexity. We compli-
cate our jobs.

Some argue that there is considerable self-gain for some
bureaucrats in building a "paper jungle" and in obsfuscating
organizational structure:

(1) It may serve as a device to keep certain persons from gaining
access to some product or service.

(2) It may cloud and frustrate any attempt to understand and
evaluate the real productivity and efficiency of the
organization.

(3) It may solidify and enhance the power of certain persons
in the organization.

(4) It may serve to frustrate or abort any sudden or major
changes in the organization.

These are probably not infrequent motivations behind the design
of much bureaucratic practice; however, for the most part, it seems
that complexity is built out of a base of good intentions. As we
are repeatedly told, these many requirements of organizational life
have been established for our own good and protection. Without the
extensive manual material, we are assured that public welfare would
be inundated by "welfare cheaters" and sloppy worker performances.

The question really boils down to whether the large bureaucracy
allows us to use organizations as tools, or does it bury us in complicated busy work? This question is, unfortunately, answered by the

establishment of our newest social invention - advocacy. There is perhaps no greater irony in the organization of human services than the advocacy phenomena. We have purportedly created the most productive and efficient institutions in human civilization; yet, there has never been greater organized effort on the part of consumers to "protect themselves" and to force entry into a system through the maze of the system's complexities. In the western frontier of the 1800's, we hired guns for personal protection; today we hire "advocates". Even the large organizations themselves openly acknowledge the need for advocates when they provide resources to fund them. (Though admittedly this could be a subtle smoke screen to direct attention from the fundamental defect of the organizational model itself).

The institution we created to care for people and to help people care for themselves, indulges itself with organizational complexity, and then tries to resolve its dilemma through benevolent advocacy strategies. We now have children's advocates, senior citizen advocates, poverty advocates. We set up a web of rules and workers to catch child abusers; then we hire an advocate to defend the person caught in our web. We institutionalize a mentally ill person and then hire an advocate to be vigilant about the advisability of institutionalization. Social workers theorize their roles as institution brokers, helping the poor and unfortunate persons muddle their ways through red tape and bureaucratic disinterest. A few make it; many, sadly, do not. It would seem that "advocacy" is society's grandest cop-out. It lacks the capacity to imagine or even dream of alternatives to humanize organizations to such an extent that advocates are not needed.

(1) Never use one word when a dozen will suffice. (2) If
it can be understood it's not yet finished. (3) Never do
anything for the first time.

   Smith's Principles of Bureaucratic Tinkertoys

A third tool of human service organizations is language. Since our profession focuses on working with people, interpersonal communication becomes our most necessary tool. But how do we communicate? Not well. It seems at times that we actually use language that belittles our clients. At the least, it confuses without enlightening them. Pretentious language, as well as the rules, regulations, procedures, and protocols are perceived as barricades against gaining access to the agency's inner chambers. Only insiders seem to know and understand how to make the organization work and how to read and speak the language of the professionals.

It does seem that we use language to set ourselves apart from clients. The elderly woman talking with the intake worker needs help, but we ask her to specify what she wants - SSI, DDI, Title XIX, an ATP card, Social Security - what? Perhaps she needs to see a protective services worker, a counselor, an advocate, a friend of the court. Would she be more comfortable with Adlerian, TA, PAC, STEP, Reality Therapy, RET - what? We do love our words - especially those that don't mean anything until one can translate them into the phrases the letters represent.

We agree with George Orwell that English usage has reached a low. Our speech is pretentious - filled with jargon that hides sloppy thinking. Only experts can tell us what our manuals say. The line worker must have each paragraph carefully explained, but s/he lacks the time to explain it to his/her client. What could be a much simpler system is complicated by pretentious language. Orwell gives the example of the quote from Ecclesiastes:

> I returned and saw under the sun, that the
> race is not to the swift, nor the battle
> to the strong, neither yet bread to the wise,
> nor yet riches to men of understanding, nor yet favor
> to men of skill; but time and chance
> happeneth to them all.

Here it is in modern English:

> Objective consideration of contemporary pheno-
> mena compels the conclusion that success or
> failure in competitive activities exhibits
> no tendency to be commensurate with innate
> capacity, but that a considerable element of
> the unpredictable must invariably be taken
> into account.[5]

Doesn't the second paragraph sound familiar? It could be a part

of some human services manual.

An organization can be either a democratic tool or a demogogic

tool. When it loses its personality and takes on the face of a

"system", it falls into the demogogic category. Nothing can push

an organization into demogogery more quickly than language. When

a child gets a label of DD, gifted and talented, hyperactive, LP,

MD, ER, smart - any label, s/he ceases to be a person and becomes

the label. When a client becomes a UM, a single parent, a divorcee,

a welfare mother, a junkie, an alcoholic - whatever, s/he exchanges

personal identity for a place in the "system". Our stilted language

deprives us of the humanness of working together, and it converts

a tool into a hindrance.

Is it any wonder that what was to have been our tools becomes

a contributor to bureau neurosis? Are we surprised that people fail

to identify with our social institutions? Institutional loyalty

is a joking matter to most employees. How can one identify with something that one cannot understand or comprehend? Institutions become some kind of complex thing which holds an awesome measure of influence over our well-being, but as individuals these organizations are beyond our control. Lacking the belief that we can influence it, many quit trying. This alone is reason to argue for simplification of all aspects of organizational life.

Perhaps no one has attacked the phenomena of bureaucratic organizational complexity and the destruction of tools more directly than Ivan Illich, noted social theological scholar. In his book, Tools for Conviviality Illich presents both his criticism of the direction of post-industrial developments and shares his concept of an alternative future.

By convivial Illich means tools which are simple, intelligible and accessible to average human use. It is technology within human scale and reach. It is concepts and instruments that can be easily and inexpensively used, with minimal instruction, by the vast majority of people, irrespective of income and education. Illich's preoccupation was the maldistribution of "power" that resulted in a world of high technology which made professionals/technocrats the high priests of technology.[6]

Insofar as Illich's concept covers "laws and organizational procedures", it can be drawn upon as the theoretical base for our alternative organizational principle - organizational conviviality and simplicity. Organizations must not be designed to make people dependent, but to free them. They must not be designed as tools

that are of use only when "experts" serve as essential intermediaries.
The ideal is to create organizations that have:

1) simple organizational structures

2) minimal rules and regulations

3) understandable procedures and practices

4) limited need for secondary accountability and control

5) intelligible professionals who speak basic English

and are identified with the clientele.

To the hard-nosed managers of today, the pious pleadings of
the Ivan Illich's are treated as quixotic, nineteenth century romantic
pipedreams. He is accused of being unwilling and unable to match
wits with the post-industrial underbelly of the nation. Today's
professional, equipped with the tools of high technology, welcomes
the design of a world that bestows them with power and privilege
over the vast majority. The generations now in power know only a
world of large corporations, complex organizations and managerial
elites. While they admit to imperfections in the bureaucratic model,
they assume solutions rest in more of the same - more technology,
more complexity, more regulations, more rational design.

Through simplification of organizational models and protocols,
we can find out who is hiding in the crevices of the organization,
and who is crouched behind the "paper mountain". We need a commitment
to humanocracy, a commitment to simplify our tools to "give each
person who uses them the greatest opportunity to enrich the environment
with the fruits of his or her vision."[7] We need to add humanocracy

to bureaucracy by replacing complicated organizational structures and processes with convivial tools.

Chapter XI

Notes

1. Ivan Illich, _Tools for Conviviality_ (New York: Harper and Row, 1974).

2. Herbert Kaufman, _Red Tape: Its Origin, Uses and Abuses_ (Washington, D.C.: The Brookings Institution, 1977), p. 1.

3. From the movie, "Gone With the Wind".

4. Virginia Robinson, _A Changing Psychology of Social Casework_ (Chapel Hill: University of North Carolina Press, 1930).

5. George Orwell, "Politics and the English Language," from _Shooting an Elephant and Other Essays_ (New York: Harcourt Brace Jovanovich, Inc., 1945).

6. Ivan Illich.

7. Illich, p. 21.

154

CHAPTER XII

ACTION STEPS FOR IMPLEMENTING PRINCIPLES OF

HUMANOCRACY PRINCIPLES

We arrive at this final chapter not knowing the extent to which the reader may have agreed or disagreed with the concepts and principles that have been presented. Assuming there has been some agreement with our analysis of the deficiencies of the hard-line bureaucratic management model, there remains the most critical question: Can humanocracy be implemented? Is it a truly viable alternative to bureaucracy in a human service organization? Can it work?

Before we begin to tackle this key question, it is necessary to clarify our position. Modern management is not all bad. It has definitely introduced some necessary reforms in the operation of large organizations. Management science has certainly made us aware of the potential of new electronic media (e.g. computers, word processing, etc.). It has sensitized us to the importance of accountability and cost effectiveness. It has brought to our attention that help for the needy is public matter. We do not feel that humanocracy in any way negates these considerations.

However, when economies of scale become diseconomies of scale or when institutional ends become displaced, we must call a halt to the organizational model that is its cause. Humanocracy is a necessary ballast to what has happened to large organizational life.

Obviously we can no longer tolerate the continued alienation of people from their institutions, particularly when these institutions have as their goal the care and consolation of troubled people in society.

Humanocracy for the writers is not just a grand theory; it is the practical application of social work knowledge and values to the administration of social welfare agencies. For us, the principles are tested principles. For the past five years, the authors were associated with a graduate school of social work which implemented each of the presented principles as the basis of the administration of the school. This field test proved that while there are definite adjustment problems in shifting from one model of administration to another, the concepts are very workable in the long run. After five years the school was considered to be one of the most interesting, productive units of the university, characterized further by exceptionally high student morale. Admittedly, a university setting is probably not your "classic bureaucracy"; but, nonetheless, the school was a relatively large program in a university of 25,000 students. During this same period, several neighboring county welfare units also worked on implementing humanocratic procedures.

Change is always difficult. Rarely does it occur without some real measure of discontentment with the way things are. If all is well in your organization -- workers are satisfied, clients are well served and the work is proceeding productively -- then no change is indicated.

If, however, it is quite apparent to everyone that there exists some deep-seated dissatisfaction with the work life, turnover and absentee rates are high, and client frustration with the service is apparent, then the first action step should begin. Namely, talk about it.

TALK ABOUT IT

The most reasonable thing to do when organizational life isn't going well is to simply stop things for a moment and talk about it. Air frustrations, either formally or informally. Solicit analysis from all levels (management, workers, clients) as to why the work experience is not proceeding well.

If the administration is sensitive to the issues and comfortable with this sort of tension, a more formal series of meetings can be held. If they take a hard line and/or skirt the issue, then those who feel the problem is real should discuss it informally.

Related to simply the airing of frustration is the discussion of alternatives. If you are serious about introducing a new mode of administration along the line of humanocracy, then study the model carefully. Understand fully the proposed "alternative ideas" in the discussion. All constituencies will eventually need to be "felt out" as to their views about organizational change. There may, of course, be full agreement on some principles and not on others. And while they logically seem to hang together as an integrated model, don't be afraid of some sort of compromise in which one or two principles are worked on. It's better to begin in modest increments

with strong consensus, than to be so "principled" that you anger
the forces of resistance.

Perhaps this book could serve as a study guide for the proposed
type of discussions. There may also be consultants or speakers who
could be invited to address some of the issues. Persons from the
human relations or industrial relations field frequently share many
of the humanocratic principles.

It is important in these discussions to build a plan of action,
to set some goals and a timetable (note such rational planning is
as much a humanocratic process as a modern management process).
As with all good theories about social change, select goals that
are simple, reasonable and can be readily accomplished. It should
be possible for each person to get a personal sense of accomplishment.

PERSONALIZE YOUR SPACE

For this reason, we suggest doing something positive to your
environment. Hopefully this can be done within the rules. Where
you feel uncertain about what you can or cannot do, don't ask. Just
do it. If what you're doing doesn't cost anything or doesn't incon-
venience someone else, it will probably not become an issue.

The underlying concept in making a personal "impression" on
your environment is, of course, to put a little more of the private,
personal you into your work life and environment. You redefine yourself in ways that make you more than the old job description. Like
the Honduran cab driver who decorates his cab, everyone from the
secretary to the computer programmer should add a little touch of home

to the tools of their trade. Certainly the desk areas, shelving areas, etc. can lean toward becoming more "homelike".

The same might be said of one's costume - clothing. Look around you. How stereotyped is one's dress? Does there appear to be unspecified hidden conversation regarding wearing apparel? Have we become uniformed without knowing it? Quite possible, of course, your organization does in fact require a uniform. If not, then express as much of yourself as you can through this physical dimension. To be comfortably clothed, acknowledging accepted standards, adds to the sense of control over one's most immediate environment.

There remains the common spaces -- the corporate areas. The open spaces in the organization seem not to belong to anyone in particular, other than the system. Hence they reflect even more the benign neglect and sterility which the bureaucratic "architect" inevitably seems to produce. The common areas must be viewed as the corporate homestead, areas crying to be taken over for purposes of development. Since the areas belong to no one, no one person really dares to do much with them. Collective action, however, can. The "office" can get together and talk about what can be done to fix up the waiting area or the coffee room or the endless corridor. Ideally some changes can be made with little cost and with volunteer labor from the office staff itself. Needless to say, many good ideas will not be possible because one cannot overcome the supervisory veto or some bureaucratic regulations. Again, take the easiest route possible, do the non-offensive and non-threatening changes first. If they wear well with most of the staff, they will welcome further experimentation.

I think back to a summer program for high school students I had

once where we were given an empty room in an old vacated building

without even chairs to sit on. By the next morning we had transformed

the environment completely without spending a cent. How? Each student

was requested to bring an important, highly personal artifact from

his or her home and a chair. The effect was marvelous. Rocking

chairs, stuffed Panda bears, straight back chairs, captain's chairs --

a wide range were added to our heretofore empty space. My students

became their own people. We also proved to be a highly productive

group of teachers and learners, as well as people who learned of,

and respected, another's personhood.

FORM A COMMITTEE

Oh no, falling back to the old bureaucratic strategy? No, not

really. The committee which we have in mind is a full constituent

governance body. In the larger organization, it is a representative

body elected from the various contingency groups. Its function is

to provide for decision-making impact from all sections of the organiza-

tion in all decisions that would affect the well-being of any member

of one of the constituencies.

This doesn't mean the organization is run by committee. It does

mean, however, that there are some issues that are of deep concern to

staff and clients which require the opportunity to have both a say and

a vote.

Administrative procedures and personnel policies are often of

vital concern to staff, as are program policies for clients. The power of administration and policy-makers to allocate resources and run the organization are not arbitrary powers. In the spirit of humanocracy, such power needs to be broadly vested in those whose lives may be affected by the decisions. From our vantage point, social welfare organizations (as social institutions) belong to everyone who chooses (or is chosen) to associate with them.

As we suggested earlier in the book, the bureaucratic organization has made a fiction of democracy. We talk a good game of "input", but what we really mean is you give us the "input" data, and a few of us with our machines will make the decision. This has become the pervading condition of our times and has invented its own label -- technocracy.

So step three is to form a little committee, discuss the issues which you feel are important to your welfare, and then let democracy take its course. Don't be surprised if there is suspicion and mistrust at the outset. People in our society haven't had a lot of practical experience in functioning in a democracy. The issues may not be the ones you'd like. And too often, a vocal few will try to dictate their own private agenda, yet that is what democracy is all about. As has been said, it's not a perfect political model, but it certainly beats any of the alternatives.

GET IT DOWN TO SIZE

The next step is one that is not so easily achieved, yet is fundamental to the implementation of nearly all of the principles --

implementing human scale. You don't have to solve a problem if you can prevent it.

How do we get an agency down to size? Once the corporate giant has been built, can it be reduced? Given all of its capital investment, can we afford not to use it even when it doesn't "fit"? Is Small really Beautiful or was E. F. Schumacher simply a frustrated small town, country boy economist?[1] Is there really an optimum size for organization if people are to give and get something from each other besides a paycheck? We have taken the position that there is such a thing as human scale and the corporate world (albeit finance, government or social welfare) has grown beyond such limits.

So we suggest the committee think through a plan to "unitize" all sectors of the organization or the organization itself into human scale-sized sub-organizations. This is admittedly no easy matter. Any major organizational reform usually takes a minimum of two years lead time to complete. With everything, however, there must be a beginning.

Unitization will have its critics. It means not only developing small scale units, but it also requires the ability to function as a unit -- with some modest degree of autonomy and independence. It willingly distributes power away from the center and spreads it in a more balanced way throughout the organization.

How can it be done? In a social welfare setting part of it is simply doing it -- one rents five small spaces rather than one large space. However, five spaces can be inefficient if it means that a person has to go five different places to get one service. So the units must be basically complete -- able to produce the total product. The work consequently needs to be reorganized and the tools redesigned to fit the smaller shop.

We are at a point where, at least in the social welfare field, we need shops, not factories; craftsmen, not technocrats; and some handmade items in lieu of mass-produced, standardized projects. This should be the nature of social welfare -- the only remaining institution, other than the family, to be kept at a human scale.

CHANGE LEADERSHIP STYLES AND EVALUATION MODES

To be without leadership is anarchy, so what we next need to implement is a different style of leadership. First, there is a need for as much sharing of leadership as possible. How can it be distributed up and down the line? There are never too many chiefs, if we recognize that the chiefs are also Indians.

People need some status and position. If it is not overly scarce, it can be more readily shared; therefore, we recommend giving a lot of people a little authority and avoid giving a few people a lot of authority. Giving staff authority is tantamount to giving staff responsibility. Few people act responsibly if they are not given the occasions to do so.

Accountability, the newest preoccupation of the bureaucracy, must be designed so that it is conducted from within the person, not from within the system. The emphasis on accountability through surveillance techniques that we have designed is costly. The costs are threefold -- they take time away from service to clients, they require administra-

tive overhead, and they tend to be demoralizing to the staff being
scrutinized.

In some ways institutional accountability is an artifact of
"bigness". Administrators in large organizations did not know workers
and, being too far removed from their direct activities, these
bureaucrats were forced to invent a mode of paper assurance that
staff were doing what they were supposed to do. The paper controls,
however, inevitably backfire. They become ends rather than means.
They become a game without substance. In the end, they are self-
defeating.

At the human scale we operate on a trust level and a more personal
identification level. Both the quantity and quality of our work are
readily apparent to supervisors and co-workers. Collegial relationships insure an important level of peer control. Consumer and policy
maker awareness of what is going on is also more easily added into
the accountability process.

Leadership in a humanocratic organization comes from one's personal
qualities and performances, not from the arbitrariness of position.
Implementation of this leadership model requires acceptance of the
model by those in administratively responsible positions. Beyond
this, however, it requires a new approach to performance evaluation.
The committee concerned with introducing humanocratic principles
would need to introduce procedures for this type of performance
evaluation. As previously outlined, what is required is a mechanism
for assuring that the "governed" are able to evaluate the "governing".
All performance evaluations must include evaluative statements from

those who are affected by the work performance of the person being evaluated. Authority of position is thus validated by evidence of merit in carrying out the responsibilities of that assignment.

Given the focus of bureaucracy in the establishment of a humane working environment, it will be necessary to include in the performance evaluation information about the contributions of the person evaluated to the working environment. This would help us sensitize workers at all levels to their collective impact on each other's well-being.

PERSONALIZE YOUR RELATIONSHIPS

Implementation of humanocracy requires an increase of face-to-face communication and a decrease of secondary and written communication. At a minimum, administrative personnel will need to communicate in more personal and direct ways with line workers and lower echelon staff. There is no magic to this suggestion, other than to begin the practice. In our own experience, we found that placing a surcharge on memo writing helped to draw attention to the issue. The Director of the School of Social Work set an example by charging himself $1.00 for every memo sent to his faculty, with proceeds going to fund the office Christmas party. He also established his office in an open area in the reception room and located his desk near the faculty mailbox. This resulted in daily face-to-face contact with the majority of his staff.

While many administrators may feel reluctance at giving up the privacy and security of well fortified offices, such habits are inimical to the modern need for more direct communication in organizational life. There needs to be private work areas, but these can be common study carrells that can be used by all employees, including top management, on an as-needed basis.

For the skeptical administrator, we'd only ask that there be a trial experiment in moving into the field of more direct activity of the agency. Be seen frequently. Even in medicine, doctors have learned the importance of making daily rounds. Administrators of social agencies need to begin following similar practices.

SIMPLIFY THE PROCEDURES

The final proposed action step is both simple and complicated. Everybody agrees that we have made a mockery of our service giving and caring activities by inventing a massive paper blockade. There is only one action we can take to make our services truly accessible -- make it simple to get them. We could begin by sunsetting the most ridiculous policies and procedures that are currently in the books. Then we could establish a "ceiling" of how much verbiage (often verbal garbage) we place in the way of getting our work done.

Obviously, much of the paper blockage is imposed upon us and there may not be much we can immediately do about this. Our job is simply to insure that we haven't added to it. We need to control that which is in our control and deal with the rest through orderly procedures.

Perhaps we need a "paper impact" statement (very short, please) at the end of each year, letting those above us in the service hierarchy know what is worth knowing and what is senseless information gathering.

In simplifying our organizational life, more than policies and procedures need to be reduced to manageable and intelligible scale. We must also simplify organizational structure. Applying the principle of functional generalization will help immensely in this process. We have overdesigned our organizations to the point that they are really no longer within control. The structure controls us and robs us of our best service instincts.

So there it is. You decide. Have we presented a pipe dream or a plan to rationalize and humanize the most important institution in our society? Let's not waste any more time; simply get about the business of life -- living and working in a humane and dignified way.

SENIOR BUREAUCRAT IS READY
AT ALL TIMES FOR DYNAMIC INACTION

Chapter XII

Notes

1. E. F. Schumacher, <u>Small is Beautiful.</u> <u>Economics as if People Mattered</u> (Toronto: Bantam Books, 1974).

Thanks are owed to many folks in getting this manuscript into its final form. As typically happens, the authors walk away from most of the dirty details of getting materials into a publishable format. We owe a special thank you to Mary Duffy our editorial assistant, Roxanne Miller our excellent typist, and Jayne Dinsmore who had the unfortunate task of typing the rough copy from our near illegible hand scrawling.

The authors.

INDEX

BIBLIOGRAPHY

Albers, Henry, Principles of Organization and Management, New York: John Wiley and Sons, Inc., 1965.

Alexander, Chauncey, "Management of Human Service Organizations", Encyclopedia of Social Work, 17th Issue, 1977, NASW, Washington, D.C.

Allport, Gordon and Leo Postman, The Psychology of Rumor, New York: Henry Holt & Co., 1947.

Allport, Gordon, Becoming, New Haven: Yale University Press, 1955.

Argyris, Chris, "Leadership Pattern in the Plant", Readings in Industrial and Business Psychology, Harry W. Karn and B. Von Haller Gilmer, Eds., New York: McGraw-Hill Book Company, Inc., 1962.

Aviriam, Uri, "Institutions and Their Changing Environment: Structures and Processes for Adaptation", Administration in Social Work, V. 3, No. 1, Spring 1979.

Bell, Daniel, The Coming of Post-Industrial Society, New York: Basic Books, Inc., 1976.

Biggerstaff, Marilyn, "The Administrator and Social Agency Evaluation", Administration in Social Work, Vol. 1, No. 1, Spring 1977.

Blau, Peter M., Bureaucracy in Modern Society, New York: Random House, 1965.

Bobbitt, Randolph, et. al., Organizational Behavior - Understanding and Prediction, Englewood Cliffs, NJ: Prentice Hall, Inc., 1978.

Boettcher, Richard, "The Service Delivery System: What Is It?", Public Welfare, Vol. 32, No. 1, Winter 1974.

Boren, James, When In Doubt, Mumble, New York: Van Nostrand Reinhold Co., 1972.

Brager, George and Stephen Holloway, Changing Human Service Organizations, New York: The Free Press, 1978.

Burns, Tom, "The Directions of Activity and Communication in a Departmental Executive Group", Human Relations, 7, 1954.

Case, R.W. and R. Boren, The Human Transaction, Glenview, IL: Scott Foresman Co., 1973.

Champion, Dean, The Sociology of Organizations, New York: McGraw-Hill Book Co., 1975.

Chaplin, Charlie, City Lights, 1931.

Chase, Andrew B., Jr., "How to Make Downward Communication Work", Personnel Journal, 49 (6), 1970.

Cherns, Albert, "The Principles of Sociotechnical Design", Human Relations, Vol. 29, No. 8, 1976.

Cohen, Neil A. and Gary B. Rhodes, "Social Work Supervision: A View Toward Leadership Style and Job Orientation in Education and Practice", Administration in Social Work, Vol. 1, No. 3, Fall 1977.

Daley, Michael R., "'Burnout' Smoldering Problem in Protective Services", Social Work, Vol. 24, No. 5, September 1979.

Davis, Keith, Organizational Behavior - A Book of Readings, New York: McGraw-Hill Book Co., 1975.

Davis, Louis E., "Evolving Alternative Organizational Designs: Their Sociotechnical Bases", Human Relations, Vol. 30, No. 3, 1977.

Delbecq, Andre and Ladbrook, Dennis, "Administrative Feedback on the Behavior of Subordinates", Administration in Social Work, Vol. 3, No. 2, Summer 1979

DeWhirst, H.D., "Influence of Perceived Information Sharing Norms on Communication Channel Utilization", Academy of Management Journal, 14, 1971.

DeWolfson, Bruce H., "Public Sector MBO and PPB: Cross Fertilization in Management Systems", Public Administration Review, 35 (4), 1975.

Downs, Anthony, Inside Bureaucracy, Boston: Little, Brown and Co., 1967.

Drucker, Peter, Practice of Management, New York: Harper & Row, 1954.

Elbow, Margaret, "On Becoming an Executive Director", Social Casework, 56 (9), November 1975.

Elgin, Duane S. and Robert A. Bushness, "The Limits to Complexity: Are Bureaucracies Becoming Unmanageable?", The Futurist, December 1977.

Emery, Frederick Edmund and E.L. Trist, Towards a Social Ecology, London: Plenum Press, 1973.

Etzioni, Amitai, A Comparative Analysis of Complex Organizations, New York: Free Press, 1964.

Fayol, Henri, General and Industrial Management, Trans. Constance Starrs, London: Pitman, 1949.

Franklin, Michael L. "A Practical Guide to Service System Reorganization", Administration in Social Work, Vol. 2, No. 1, Spring 1978.

Freelander, William, "Some Considerations in the Design of Public Social Service Systems", Public Welfare, October 1970.

Galbraith, John Kenneth, Economics and the Public Purpose, Boston: Houghton Mifflin, 1973.

Gamson, William, Power and Discontent, Homewood, IL: The Dorsey Press, 1968.

Gibb, Jack R., "Defensive Communication", The Journal of Communication, II (3), 1961.

Gilbert, Neil, "Assessing Service Delivery Methods: Some Unsettled Questions", Welfare in Review, 10 (3), 1972.

Gillespie, David F. and Susanne E. Marten, "Assessing Service Accessibility", Administration in Social Work, Vol. 2, No. 2, Summer 1978.

Gilmore, Thomas, "Managing Collaborative Relationships in Complex Organizations", Administration in Social Work, Vol. 3, No. 2, Summer 1979.

Goffman, Erving, Asylums, Garden City, New York: Doubleday & Company, Inc., 1961.

Graham, Robert and Milton Valentine, "Management Communication and the Destandardized Man", Personnel Journal, 52 (11), 1973.

Granvold, Donald K., "Supervisory Style and Educational Preparation of the Public Welfare Supervisor", Administration in Social Work, Vol. 1, No. 1, Spring 1977.

Grusky, Oscar and George Miller, The Sociology of Organizations - Basic Studies, New York: The Free Press, 1970.

Haas, Eugene and Thomas Drabek, Complex Organizations, New York: The Macmillan Publishers, 1973.

Hawthorne, Lillian, "Games Supervisors Play", Social Work, 20 (3), 1975.

Herbst, P. G., Technical Design, London: Tavistock Publications Limited, 1974.

Hersey, Paul and Kenneth Blanchard, Management of Organizational Behavior, Englewood Cliffs, New Jersey: Prentice-Hall, Inc., 1972.

Hill, Michael, The Sociology of Public Administration, New York: Crane, Russak & Company, Inc., 1972.

Horejsi, John E., Thomas Walz and Patric R. Connolly, Working in Welfare: Survival Through Positive Action, Iowa City, Iowa: University of Iowa School of Social Work, 1977.

Houy, Julia, "Ramblings", from Liguorian, reprinted in Elizabeth Ferguson, Social Work, Philadelphia: J. B. Lippincott Company, 1975.

Hummel, Ralph, The Bureaucratic Experience, New York: St. Martin's Press, 1977.

Hurst, J. C. and Davidshafer M. Moore and U. Delworth, "Agency Directionality and Staff Individuality", Personnel and Guidance Journal, 54 (6), February 1976.

Illich, Ivan, Tools for Conviviality, New York: Harper and Row, Publishers, 1973.

Jacobsen, Eugene and Stanley Seashore, "Communication Practices in Complex Organizations", Journal of Social Issues, 7, 1951.

Johns, Edward, The Sociology of Organizational Change, New York: Pergamon Press, 1973.

Jorge, Antonio, Competition, Cooperation, Efficiency and Social Organization, Rutherford: Fairleigh Dickinson University Press, 1978.

Jun, Jong, Tomorrow's Organizations: Challenges and Strategies, Glenview, IL: Scott, Foresman and Co., 1973.

Katz, Daniel and Robert Kahn, The Social Psychology of Organizations, New York: John Wiley & Sons, Inc., 1966.

Kaufman, Herbert, Red Tape: Its Origin, Uses and Abuses, Washington, D.C.: The Brookings Institution, 1977.

Kelley, Joe, Organizational Behavior, Homewood, IL: Richard D. Irwin, Inc., 1974.

Kerson, Toba Schwabauer, and Leslie B. Alexander, "Strategies for Success: Women in Social Service Administration", Administration in Social Work, Vol. 3, No. 3, Fall 1979.

Kimberly, John, et.al., The Organizational Life Cycle, San Francisco: Jossey-Bass Publishers, 1980.

Klein, Stuart and Richard Ritti, Understanding Organizational Behavior, Boston: Kent Publishing Co., 1980.

Koehler, Jerry W. and Karl W. E. Anatol and Ronald I. Applbaum, "Communication: Environments in the Organization", Organizational Communication, Holt, Rinehart and Winston: New York: 1976.

Kriesberg, Louis, The Sociology of Social Conflicts, Englewood Cliffs, NJ: Prentice-Hall, Inc., 1973.

LeMasters, E. E., Blue Collar Aristocrats, Madison, Wisconsin: The University of Wisconsin Press, 1975.

Lessing, Doris, Going Home, New York: Popular Library, 1957.

Levin, Edward, Levin's Laws, New York: M. Evans and Company, Inc., 1980.

Levy, Charles, "The Ethics of Management", Administration in Social Work, Vol. 3, No. 3, Fall 1979.

Lewis, Harold, "The Future Role of the Social Service Administrator", Administration in Social Work, Vol. 1, No. 2, Summer 1977.

Maier, Norman R. F., "Assets and Liabilities in Group Problem Solving: The Need for an Integrative Function", Psychological Review, 1967.

March, James and Herbert Simon, Organizations, New York: John Wiley and Sons, Inc., 1966.

Maslach, Christina, "Burn Out, A High Price for Caring", The National Observer, July 11, 1977.

McGregor, Douglas M., "The Human Side of Enterprises", Readings in Personnel Management, Eds. Herbert J. Cruden and Arthur W. Sherman, Jr., Cincinnati: South Western Publishing Co., 1966.

Meinert, Robert G., "Future Forecasting", Social Work, 18 (6), 1973.

Michael, Stephens, et. al., Techniques of Organizational Change, New York: McGraw-Hill Book Co., 1981.

Mohan, Raj, Management and Complex Organizations in Comparative Perspective, Westport, CT: Greenwood Press, 1979.

Mullis, Scott, "Management Applications to the Welfare System", Public Welfare, 33 (4), 1975.

Olmstead, C. B., "Some Management Principles of Staffing Social Welfare Organizations", Social Work, Vol. 6, No. 3, July 1961.

Orwell, George, "Politics and the English Language", from Shooting an Elephant and Other Essays, New York: Harcourt Brace Jouanovich, Inc., 1945.

Ottaway, Richard, Change Agents at Work, Westport, CT: Greenwood Press, 1979.

Parsons, Jack R. "Collegial Administration as a Model for Social Agencies", Social Casework, 57 (2), 1976.

Patti, Rino, "From Direct Service to Administration: A Study of Social Workers Transition from Clinical to Management Roles", Administration in Social Work, Vol. 3, No. 2, Summer 1979.

Pawlak, Edward J. "Organizational Tinkering", Social Work, September 1976.

Perrow, Charles, Complex Organizations, A Critical Essay, Scott, Glenview, IL: Scott Foresman & Co., 1972.

Persig, Robert M., Zen and the Art of Motorcycle Maintenance, Toronto: Bantam Books, 1974.

Peter, Dr. Laurence J. and Raymond Hull, The Peter Principle. Why Things Always Go Wrong, New York: Bantam Books, 1972.

Plant, Earl and William Machaver, "Upward Communications: A Project in Executive Development", Personnel, 28-4, 1952.

Pruger, Robert, "The Good Bureaucrat", Social Work, Vol. 18, No. 4, July 1973.

Reichert, Kurt, "The Drift toward Entrepreneurialism in Health and Social Welfare: Implications for Social Work Education", Administration in Social Work, Vol. I, No. 2, Summer 1977.

Resnick, Herman, "Tasks in Changing the Organization from Within (COFW)", Administration in Social Work, Vol. 2, No. 1, Spring 1978.

Rhode, John G., et.al., "Human Resource Accounting: A Critical Assessment", Industrial Relations, 15 (1), 1976.

Robinson, Virginia, A Changing Psychology of Social Casework, Chapel Hill: University of North Carolina Press, 1930.

Rudolph, Clare S., "New Approaches to Educating Social Work Professionals for Administrative Roles in a National Health System", Social Work in Health Care, Vol. 3 (4), Summer 1978.

Ruoss, Meryl, Citizen Power and Social Change, New York: The Seabury Press, 1968.

Ryan, Robert M. and Robert O. Washington, "New Patterns for Organizing Human Services", Administration in Social Work, Vol. 1, No. 3, Fall 1977.

Sarri, Rosemary, "Administration in Social Welfare", Encyclopedia of Social Work, NASW, Washington D.C., 17 Issues, 1977.

Schumacher, E. F., Small is Beautiful, Economics as if People Mattered, New York: Harper Colophon Books, 1975.

Scott, William and David Hart, Organizational America, Boston: Houghton Miffin Co., 1979.

Smith, Gilbert, Social Work and the Sociology of Organizations, London: Routledge and Kegan Paul, 1970.

Snyder, Robert A. and Nealia S. Bruning, "Sex Differences in Perceived Competence: An Across Organization Study", Administration in Social Work, Vol. 3, No. 3, Fall 1979.

Stretch, John, "Increasing Accountability for Human Services Administrators", Social Casework, June 1978.

Sutton, H. and L. Porter, "A Study of the Grapevine in a Governmental Organization", Personnel Psychology, 21-22 (1968).

Tannebaum, Arnold S., Social Psychology of the Work Organization, Belmont, CA: Wadsworth Publishing Co., Inc., 1966.

Taylor, Frederick, Scientific Management, New York: Harper and Row, 1947.

Taylor, Howard F., Balance on Small Groups, New York: Von Nostrand, 1970.

Terkel, Studs, Working, New York: Avon, 1975.

Thayer, Lee, Communications and Communication Systems, Homewood, IL: Richard D. Irwin, 1968.

Townsend, Robert, Up the Organization, Greenwich, CT: Fawcett Publications, Inc., 1970.

Vandervelde, Maryanne, "The Semantics of Participation", Administration in Social Work, Vol. 3, No. 1, Spring 1979.

Vash, Carolyn, The Burnt-Out Administrator, New York: Springer Publishing Co., 1980.

Vonnegut, Kurt, <u>Piano Player</u>, New York: Dela Court Press, 1952.

Ward, James H., "An Approach to Measuring Effectiveness of Social Services: Problems and Resolutions", <u>Administration in Social Work</u>, Vol. 4, Winter 1977.

Weber, Shirley and Donald Palm, "Participatory Management in Public Welfare", <u>Social Casework</u>, 55 (5), 1974.

Weisman, Frederick, <u>Titticult Follies</u>, 1967; <u>Hospitals</u>, 1969; High School, 1968.

Williams, Charles W., "Managing Social Services in a Period of Rapid Change", <u>Welfare in Review</u>, 10 (3), 1972.

Williams, Robin, <u>American Society</u>, New York: Alfred A. Knopf, 1960.

York, Reginald, "Can Change be Effectively Managed?", <u>Administration in Social Work</u>, Vol. 1, No. 2, Summer 1977.

Zaleznik, Abraham, "The Human Dilemmas of Leadership", <u>Social Work Administration</u>, Harry A. Schatz, Ed., New York: Council on Social Work Education, 1970.

DATE DUE

DEC 1 9 '86			
MR 3 '87			
MY 1 '95			
MR 23 '02			